WOMEN AND TEACHING

The Madeleva Lecture in Spirituality

This series, sponsored by the Center for Spirituality, Saint Mary's College, Notre Dame, Indiana, honors annually the woman who as president of the college inaugurated its pioneering program in theology, Sister M. Madeleva, C.S.C.

1985
Monika K. Hellwig
Christian Women in a Troubled World

1986
Sandra M. Schneiders
Women and the Word

1987
Mary Collins
Women at Prayer

WOMEN AND TEACHING

*Themes for a Spirituality
of Pedagogy*

MARIA HARRIS

1988 Madeleva Lecture
in Spirituality

PAULIST PRESS
New York/Mahwah

For Joanmarie Smith, C.S.J.
Teacher extraordinary, cherished friend,
beloved Sister

Library of Congress Cataloging-in-Publication Data

Harris, Maria.
    Women and teaching / Maria Harris.
        p.   cm.
    "The Madeleva lecture in spirituality series"
    Includes bibliographical references and index.
    ISBN 0-8091-2991-4 (pbk.) : $2.95 (est.)
    1. Women's studies.   2. Teaching—Psychological aspects.
3. Teaching—Religious aspects.   4. Women—Psychology.
5. Women teachers.   I. Title.   II. Title: Madeleva lecture in spirituality series.
HQ1180.H37 1988   88-2496
305.4'07—dc19   CIP

Published by Paulist Press
997 Macarthur Blvd.
Mahwah, N.J. 07430

Printed and bound in the United States of America

Table of Contents

Introduction: Impulses.........................1

1. Silence...................................17

2. Remembering 31

3. Ritual Mourning.........................46

4. Artistry 60

5. Birthing.................................77

Notes.......................................92

Index......................................104

INTRODUCTION:
IMPULSES

On May 24, 1893, six-year-old Eva Wolff went to school for the first time. Walking into the classroom that opening day, she saw on the blackboard in careful Spencerian script the sentence, "The cat is black." An independent child, eager to get started, she took her neatly-ruled slate in her right hand, and with her left carefully began to copy. Starting from the letter k, she traced from right to left every single letter. With assurance and delight, she presented it to her new teacher. The gentle Miss Williams looked carefully, and then, with quiet directness, responded, "Oh yes, my dear. But now suppose we take the pencil in the other hand and begin at the other side of the slate and the other end of the sentence."[1]

In that brief exchange lies the initial impulse for this extended essay on the relation between women and teaching. For most women recognize that experience of little Eva Wolff, the experience of having to recast our forms of learning into molds which were not initially designed for us, into shapes and styles and sentences which often feel quite foreign.[2] At best, in the face of such forms, we move to adjustment and fine-tuning, and refuse to give up the modes of learning most fruitful for us. At worst we find ourselves left-handed people in a right-handed world, forever trying to make natural what is unnatural. And at some primeval, even mythical level, we sympathize with the mature, adult Eva—now Madeleva—musing decades later, "Even now, in hours of sleeplessness, my mind goes back to this first half-hour of school. It travels from right to left, following the first pattern of script it ever directed, repeating again and again the left-handed report, 'The cat is black.' "[3] She was remembering, as all of us do sooner or later, an original awareness, an original sense, and an original vision which held clues to who she was and who she was meant to be. And she was still questioning, after all those years, a world designed on the bases of experiences not her own.

But our sympathies are not only with Eva, the learner. They are also with Miss Williams. For she too is representative—of the thousands of teachers, women and men, who know at least fleetingly, and at best certainly, that in **not** going with the grain, in not staying with the left hand, something is being lost.[4] Some new discovery which might have been made— by this learner in this situation—is missed because of the need to conform. Miss Williams stands as our image for a teacher who wants to redesign a pedagogy which makes room for the multiple, creative capacities existing in human beings, for possibilities and processes which make for expansion, not contraction—possibilities aborted in their development before they have time to blossom.

The young Eva, and the only slightly older Miss

Williams, are therefore our initial guides in starting this exploration. The issues we will be examining begin with the conviction of disequilibrium in the situation of women and girls as students. In order to get at that disquiet, and at the proposal of a remedy, I will focus on four themes in this introduction: **teaching, women as students**, the power of **spirituality**, and the idea of **rhythm**—themes which will act as undersong for the rest of the book. This introduction will therefore be in the shape of the posing of the question; the five subsequent sections will be in the shape of one possible response.

TEACHING

The title of this book uses two words: women and teaching. I will come to "women" in a moment, but because I want to look at the relation between women and teaching, I begin with the latter here. In teaching teaching, I often suggest an exercise where I ask participants to remember three persons who taught them before they were fifteen, and three persons who have taught them in their adult lives. Although many people can remember teachers they would prefer to forget, even more can remember those in their lives (parents, storekeepers, friends as well as schoolteachers) who, by teaching them, made a permanent difference in their lives, enabling them to become who they are. Teaching is the name of a positive, universal and valued human activity. Genuine teaching occurs when someone with knowledge and skill enables and

3

empowers someone else to come into self-possession. Teachers do this by shaping and forming experience for us, so that we discover truths about ourselves and truths about our world. As one reflective person answered the question "What is Teaching?" for me, **this** is its meaning:

Teaching

We meet awkwardly.
I invite you to walk.
I find you dancing.[5]

A second word, this one in our subtitle, helps to illuminate more specific understandings of teaching, especially as we will be using it in this book. The meaning of the word **pedagogy** is inclusive of the word teaching, but specifies to the extent that pedagogy is the profession or the art of teaching; the carrying out, the practicing, the doing. Pedagogy names the philosophical work of bracketing out the work of teaching, and exploring and examining it seriously and thoroughly. In other words, pedagogy is the attentive **study** of teaching: not only with the mind but with the body's study as well. I will be drawing on this meaning in what follows, with particular attention to pedagogy as the *art* of teaching—teaching seen as a work which is, characteristically, creative, unfolding and imaginative.

Two writers who have examined pedagogy in this century have had considerable influence in religious education, although neither has given specific and extended attention to the relation between women and teaching. The first is Malcolm Knowles, who in a number of writings, notably *The Modern Practice of Adult Education*,[6] has demonstrated continuing concern for the adult learner, calling adult learners "a neglected species."[7] Knowles is rightly troubled by the equation of education with schooling, and even more so by the equation of "learner" or "student" with child. To get at this concern, he posits **two** forms of teaching—one called "pedagogy," the other called "andragogy." In setting forth his meanings of pedagogy, Knowles draws on the Greek etymology of the word, **gogus** plus **pais**: "one who leads or trains" a *pais* or child (actually a boy). From this he proposes that pedagogy is a system of teaching where (a) the role of the learner is by definition dependent; (b) the teacher is expected by society to take full responsibility for determining what is to be learned; and (c) the experience people bring to a learning situation is of little worth. In opposition to this, Knowles suggests a science of teaching which he calls "andragogy," where a person moves from dependency toward increasing self-directedness, where the learners feel a need to learn, and where the learning environment is characterized by physical comfort, mutual trust and respect, mutual helpfulness, freedom of expression and acceptance of differences.[8]

I sympathize with Knowles' concerns, but I believe his distinction can be harmful. For what he refers to as *pedagogy* is not suitable for children, boy-children **or** girl-children, any more than it is for adults. In attending to older people, Knowles tends to downplay the need for independence and mutuality in children too. But the real danger is not only the set of concerns named in Knowles' "pedagogy" but the positing of two forms of teaching, with the accompanying assumption that pedagogy (so-called) can not and ought not also lead to freedom, mutuality and the fullness of learning.

In contrast, the work of Paulo Freire, Brazilian educator, is a celebration of pedagogy. In his classic and monumental work, *Pedagogy of the Oppressed*,[9] Freire has made a lasting contribution to the meaning of pedagogy by assuming that education is itself the practice of freedom, and therefore any genuine pedagogy is "a pedagogy which must be forged **with**, not **for** the oppressed (whether individuals or peoples) in the incessant struggle to regain their humanity."[10] For Freire, the central question of **pedagogy** is the question of how people can participate in developing "the pedagogy of their own liberation,"[11] referring to that liberation as an activity of childbirth,[12] a theme to which we will return later. This celebration of pedagogy in Freire's educational philosophy, in company with the idea of teaching as an art of study and practice, is the one I assume in this book. However, the particular work I want to insist on as still needing to be done is the creating of a pedagogy appropriate to the lives of women. This I take to be the work before us here.

WOMEN AS STUDENTS

During the last decades, we have seen an extraordinary reclaiming of a tradition of scholarship which goes back to Plato and Pestalozzi, to Mary Wollstone-craft and Catherine Beecher, a tradition of examining the relation between women and education. Along with writers on women and psychology, such as Jean Baker Miller, Carol Gilligan and Nancy Chodorow,[13] an extensive and growing cadre of authors and scholars are examining the ways in which women are educated as well as the philosophies which have nurtured and formed the principles of education for women. In addition, classic statements by women in our past are being rediscovered and in some cases found for the first time, and beginning to exert an influence on what we conceive education to be. Representative but by no means exhaustive of these are Jane Roland Martin's examination of Plato, Pestalozzi, and Rousseau in conversation with Mary Wollstonecraft, Catherine Beecher and Charlotte Perkins Gilman in *Reclaiming a Conversation;*[14] Mary Belenky, Blythe Clinchy, Nancy Goldberger and Jill Tarule's jointly written *Women's Ways of Knowing;*[15] the reissuing and rereading of Virginia Woolf's *A Room of One's Own*[16] and *Three Guineas;*[17] Adrienne Rich's perceptive essays, "Claiming an Education" and "Taking Women Students Seriously";[18] and Gerda Lerner's historical assistance in enabling the majority—women—to find its past.[19] Rich, for example, raises troubling, disturbing issues:

> Item: ... the university curriculum, the high-school curriculum, do not provide for women the knowledge of Womankind, whose experience has been so profoundly different from that of Mankind.[20]

Item: . . . women and men do not receive an equal education because outside the classroom women are perceived not as sovereign beings but as prey . . . [education] is occurring in a **context** of widespread images of sexual violence against women, on billboards and in so-called high art.[21]

And this:

Look at a classroom: look at the many kinds of women's faces, postures, expressions. Listen to the women's voices. Listen to the silences, the unasked questions, the blanks. Listen to the small, soft voices, often courageously trying to speak up, voices of women taught early that tones of confidence, challenge, anger, or assertiveness, are strident and unfeminine. Listen to the voices of the women and the voices of the men; observe the space men allow themselves, physically and verbally, the male assumption that people will listen even when the majority of the group is female. Look at the faces of the silent, and of those who speak. Listen to a woman groping for language in which to express what is on her mind, sensing that the terms of academic discourse are not her language, trying to cut down her thought to the dimensions of a discourse not intended for her . . . or reading her paper aloud at breakneck speed, throwing her words away, deprecating her own work by a reflex prejudgment: **I do not deserve to take up time and space.**[22]

Certainly such items are being addressed today as never before, although I remain unpersuaded by those who belittle their description as dated or no longer true. Obviously, the development of women's studies and of feminist theory is creating a body of knowledge which faces such issues, through publication, networking, and the creation of women's presses, and through the findings reported in such journals as *Signs*,[23] *Feminist Studies*,[24] and *Women's Studies International Forum*.[25] We will draw on much of this work as we continue. However, we are still at the beginning and much more needs to be done.

In particular, we need a continuing focus on the more specific areas which are present **within** education, especially on the processes and procedures through which we—women and men—can take women students seriously: administration; supervision; context; the sociology of education; the creation of new language; remedial and compensatory programs. In this essay, I am primarily concerned with such focusing. And the particular focus I wish to choose out of the much broader context of education with its numerous issues is the act of **teaching**. More to the point, in the context of this place, and on this occasion, and in honor of the woman we come to celebrate, I wish to look at teaching as a **religious** act, a sacramental act, a holy act—I want to invite us together to look at teaching as a form of spirituality. I assume that certain experiences and themes which at root are religious resonate in the lives of women, especially in women's educational lives: **stillness, artistry, childbirth, memory, mourning**. If we hold these themes before us with intelligence and attention, examining them carefully, and then dis-cover their relation to the activity of teaching, we may arrive at a spirituality which will be a gift not only to women, but to men, to children, and to all creation.

SPIRITUALITY

Meanings of spirituality abound in contemporary culture, which is, I suspect a good thing. Any reality as rich is not easily defined, limited or controlled. Indeed, it may be accurate to say that today we are not so much involved with a spirituality (singular) as we are with many spiritualities (plural), many forms for coming to encounter the dimensions of depth and mystery which permeate human life. Carol Christ speaks of spirituality today, for example, as "a new perception of the ultimate which will arise out of the discovery and recovery of women's experience."[26] Carol Ochs compares spirituality to women's experience in mothering: the "unselfing" that occurs in pregnancy and birth—a symbol for the Unselfing which can occur throughout life, where we realize that Something or Someone is more important than we are. She also stresses the need to reject the linear, progressive "structure" of stages in spirituality, and to substitute the idea of a spiritual walk for that of a spiritual journey. That keeps us from hurrying to get somewhere, and at any moment to be precisely where we should be.[27] And Rosemary Ruether suggests that in developing spirituality, we need to draw on a theology which takes seriously "the broken relations between self and body, self and others, self and nature, self and God, as creating not just false images but also broken and distorted existence."[28] Saying this she points to one of the sometimes forgotten aspects of spirituality—the search to get at the root alienation behind these broken relations, alienations which get expressed in exploitative social patterns. These are patterns of domination and silencing such as those in education, especially toward women and girls, to which spirituality impels us to attend.

Another approach to spirituality begins with a basic reality of **original blessing** in contrast to one of **original sin**.[29] This approach starts with such values as wholeness, affirmation of the body, and the wisdom in non-human nature. It also includes as essential the memory of the lives and teaching of formerly forgotten women (Mechtilde, Hildegarde. Julian). In these ways, such a spirituality calls into question the emphases in much past spirituality on fall, redemption, and sin, and on the body, especially the female body, as source of evil. This spirituality of original blessing—Creation Spirituality—contemplates life and pronounces it not a curse, but a blessing. It severely criticizes any teaching which gives preeminence to themes which instruct people in how corrupt they are or ought to think themselves instead of reminding

11

them (again, especially women) they are of divine lineage.[30]

Out of such sources, a more profound understanding emerges of how spirituality impinges on our lives as a whole, becoming a way of life and a way of being in the world which affirms—rather than denies—ourselves and our world, while always seeking to reform and reshape that world so that it will be less inhuman, less unjust. Put another way, and adding one further element, Spirituality emerges as *our way of being in the world, our way of doing whatever we do, in the light of being touched, held, delighted by and rooted in the Mystery of Divinity—whether that Divinity is called God, Goddess, Holy Wisdom, the Unnameable or simply, "Thou."*

When we come to a spirituality **of teaching**, we will examine how the act of teaching—**this** way of being in the world—is also held up to the light of the Mystery of God, since in teaching we are always engaged with spirit. For as we teach and learn, just as we do everything else, we are in the presence of something holy, something awe-full, something sacred, something more. The poet Anne Sexton perceived it this way: "I cannot walk an inch/without trying to walk to God./ I cannot move a finger without trying to touch God."[31] Her insight brought to bear on teaching suggests: We cannot say a word, we cannot read a text, we cannot write an essay without trying to walk to God, without trying to touch God, even if we are not aware of the walking, the touching.

Thus, the possibility of a spirituality of teaching reveals itself when we consider that teaching, as a human activity, **is** directed, by its very nature, toward persons developing a greater understanding of themselves and their ways of being in the world. Educator Parker Palmer affirms this view, saying that any spirituality of education is characterized by the creation of a space where obedience to truth—our own, the world's, God's truth—is practiced,[32] a place of "careful listening and responding in a conversation of free selves."[33] Returning to Ruether, we can begin to probe how teaching is a participation in divine work, and how "The Holy Wisdom who is the foundation of our being/new being does not confine us to a stifled, dependent self nor uproot us into a spirit trip outside the earth. Rather he/she leads us to the converted center, the harmonization of self and body, self and other, self and world."[34] Teaching at its best goes in this direction, for teaching at its best is the work of learning the routes of walking into and touching this converted center of harmony and wholeness.

RHYTHM

To bring teaching, women and spirituality into an ongoing conversation, I offer the theme of rhythm. In the pages to follow, at both theoretical and practical levels, I will be working from the basic truth—asserted both by modern physics and by process theology—that the core of things is not substance, it is rhythm: movement, ongoing discovery, continuing unfolding.[35] I will be acknowledging John Dewey's teaching that rhythm is the essential sign of the living creature.[36] From a universe characterized by the rhythms of rotation, revolution, seasons and tides to the human life kept flowing through waking and sleep, pulsing breath, regular heartbeat, and monthly periods, we are immersed in rhythm. At the educational level, I will be appropriating the early work of Whitehead in naming the rhythm of education: romance, precision, synthesis;[37] and I will also be drawing on the original suggestion of generative themes posed by Paulo Freire,[38] noting in passing that the idea of "theme" is allied to music.

Which brings me to the conviction which is at the core of this book: the best way to create a spirituality of teaching which liberates women is to posit and describe a series of steps, leading to and emerging from one another in a natural rhythm. The notion of steps has been pervasive in much recent religious education, from Piaget to Erikson to Kohlberg to Fowler.[39] Almost always the steps suggested are similar to those on a staircase, moving from lower to higher, and little attention has been given to the fact that religiously, there is "no ladder to the sky."[40] (Ruether: the movement is toward a **center**.) But the series of steps I want to pose in contrast are in a different form: they are as steps in a dance.[41] Using this metaphor, we can immediately draw on the power of rhythm, and study how in the work of spirituality and teaching, a more organic and human series of steps than the ladder and the staircase are those which like the dance can go backward or forward, can incorporate one another, can involve turn and re-turn, can move down as well as up, out as well as in, and be sometimes partnered, sometimes solitary. In the dance, we do not come to

14

the next step by planning it beforehand, but by doing the bodily work from which the next step **emerges**.

And so we have a series of steps, or, to use Freire's pedagogical language, a series of generative themes. But whereas he emphasizes themes which are antithetical and contain their opposites, I will emphasize another meaning of generative, by considering each theme or step as **generating** or **giving birth to** the next. At the same time, I will be drawing on the teaching that all of us live in **thematic universes**: worlds, contexts and environments shaping us even as we shape them, and calling us to particular educational tasks.

The pattern of steps I propose is not set in an invarying order, although there is a natural dynamic or progression from one to the next. Nor do I propose that once a step is finished we need never return to or repeat it. On the contrary, each step is a dwelling place which continually teaches us simply by our entering it. To return to Carol Ochs, when we are there, we are precisely where we ought to be. However, the most important aspect of these steps is that each of them is drawn from the lives and experiences of women, and each forms the familiar environment of our thematic universes. I have alluded to most of them already, but here I propose that considered in relation to one another, these themes—or steps—can give us the framework, the choreography and the basis for a women's pedagogy. They are the themes from which together we can create a spirituality of teaching. And although we do not, as I have already said, leave one behind when we go on to the next, we do turn our attention now more toward one, now more toward the other. In the next five sections, we examine each of them in turn, in the hope that when that is finished, we shall have made some discoveries. We turn now to those steps, and, one after the other, begin the movement from *Silence,* to *Remembering,* to *Ritual Mourning,* to *Artistry* and to *Birthing.* My hope is that as we do so, we will come to the realization that in the lives of women, these themes sound a sacred musical harmony. If listened to with awareness and obedience to truth, and entered with courage and community, they hold the potential of setting the world dancing in the ways it needs to go.

1:
SILENCE

It would be difficult to find a more pervasive theme in contemporary study of women than the theme of silence. In innumerable conversations as well as in essays and books, women studying women use as the starting point the experience of women's silence and the accompanying and complementary work of finding a voice. Tillie Olsen writes a series of essays entitled, "Silences";[1] Adrienne Rich speaks of "Lies, Secrets and Silences";[2] Rita Gross and Nancy Falk, writing on the religious lives of women, name them "Unspoken Worlds."[3] Carol Gilligan calls her work "In a Different Voice";[4] Jane Roland Martin names hers "Reclaiming a Conversation";[5] Theodora Penny Martin entitles hers "The Sound of Our Own Voices."[6] Exploring the emergence of women's poetry in America, Alicia Suskin Ostriker calls that experience "Stealing the Language."[7]

Perhaps the most striking example of this exploration of silence, voice and speaking comes in the study already alluded to called *Women's Ways of Knowing*.[8] In this careful research into the educational lives of over one hundred women, the authors initially relate an insight similar to ours—the universe of silence—but then go on to comment:

> What we had not anticipated was that 'voice' was more than an academic shorthand for a person's point of view. Well after we were into our interviews with women, we became aware that it is a metaphor that can apply to many aspects of women's experience and development. In describing their lives, women commonly talked about voice and silence: 'speaking up,' 'speaking out,' 'being silenced,' 'not being heard,' 'really listening,' 'really talking,' 'words as weapons,' 'feeling deaf and dumb,' 'having no words,' 'saying what you mean,' 'listening to be heard,' and so on in an endless variety of connotations all having to do with sense of mind, self-worth, and feelings of isolation from or connection to others. We found that women repeatedly used the metaphor of voice to depict their intellectual and ethical development; and that the development of a sense of voice, mind and self were intricately intertwined.[9]

These insights are incorporated so wholly into the entire scheme of the book that women's ways of knowing are subsequently characterized in the following terms: the movement toward knowledge is a rhythm from (a) Silence; to (b) Listening to the Voices of Others; to (c) the subjective knowledge of the Inner Voice; on through (d) the Quest for Self to (e) the Voice of Reason; and finally to the constructed knowledge where women are engaged in a final task of (f) "Integrating the Voices."[10] For our purposes in incorporating such findings into a spirituality of teaching, it is instructive to learn that when the writers asked themselves, concerning the women they had interviewed, "What are the problems this woman is trying to solve? What is adaptive about the way she is trying to accommodate to the world as she sees it?" and "What are the metaphors she uses to depict her experience of growing and changing?" one metaphor reverberated throughout the stories of intellectual development. Over and over, women spoke of "gaining a voice." It is small wonder then that in the thematic **educational** universe of women the first and resounding experience is that of silence. In this section we will examine silence from three aspects: *silence in the curriculum; responses to silence; silence as healing power.*

SILENCE IN THE CURRICULUM

A framework which enables us to examine this theme as it is related to teaching comes from Elliot Eisner. In *The Educational Imagination,* Eisner points out that if we look at curriculum in any depth, we discover that every institution teaches not one, but three curricula. These are the **explicit**, the **implicit** and the **null** curricula.[11] The explicit curriculum refers to what is consciously taught, what is overtly and verbally addressed, what is printed and presented as the subject matter to be studied. In contrast, the implicit curriculum is less obvious but still influential, and found in the interstices and in the atmosphere: patterns of direct address, or of decision making or of designating positions of influence. In other words, the implicit curriculum refers to "what **really** gets said" in what gets said, to "what **really** goes on"—subtly and at the margins—in what goes on, in between the lines and in the silences. It refers not only to who speaks, but more importantly to who gets heard in the "politics of talking."[12] The implicit curriculum extends also to the form and organization and patterns of discourse which shape learning, and to which patterns are valued most, for example, conversation, sermon, lecture, poetry. It also refers to the way words are put together—for example technically and abstractly in contrast to evocatively or concretely. Eisner distinguishes nicely between the explicit and implicit curricula (indicating how teachers might enable students to do the same) by citing the painter Li-li Weng: "First you see the hills in the painting; then you see the painting in the hills."[13]

And the null curriculum is third. A paradox, this is a curriculum which exists because it does not exist, for it refers to areas left out, ideas not addressed, concepts not offered. It also refers to processes and procedures (from designing a course with the participants rather than for them, to encouraging site visits to see what is being studied first-hand, to revealing insights through mime and drama) which are rarely or never employed. And the point of including the null curriculum is, of course, that ig-norance—not knowing something—is never neutral. If we do not know about something, or do not realize what is addressed can be understood in another manner or seen through another lens, it skews our viewpoint; it limits our options; it clouds our perspective. The thing which does not fit in or which is left out forcefully educates and miseducates everyone, since the thing which is left out or forgotten regularly turns out to be the clue leading to new knowledge.

Examining the three curricula in relation to the first generative theme, we have come to realize, in the last few decades, a deafening silence: silence about women, of women, by women, toward women. With reference to the explicit curriculum, for example, it has become more and more obvious that the bulk of curricular resources in philosophy, education, history, literature, religion and theology, until the very recent past, excluded the stories and experience of women, as well as the research and writing done by women. The explicit curriculum taught us of Rousseau's *Emile*,[14] but far less of his proposals for the education of Sophie, including a critique of them, until Jane Roland Martin.[15] It offered us commentary on Pestalozzi's schooling of Leonard, but what did we know of Gertrude? It taught us of Abraham, but less about Sarah, and rarely anything of Hagar.[16] It taught of Moses, but not of Miriam. We learned of the great (so-called) military leaders and the great (so-called) military battles, but what of the women who never left home?[17] Why were their stories never told? What of the conquered, the losers, the dead non-combatants? What of the proposals to **end** war found in Virginia Woolf's treatise on educating women in *Three Gui-*

neas?[18] At last, some—but by no means all—educators have begun to ask serious and sobering questions about the explicit curriculum: where are the bullets to buy back the stories of the children who will never grow old? In other words, our perusal of the explicit curricula has been the key to recognition of silence, and our own time has been one of extraordinary movement toward redressing imbalances.

Similar movement and care now faces educators examining the implicit and null curricula, a more difficult work because these curricula are more subtle. A now-classic essay of Valerie Saiving encapsulates the issue where the implicit curriculum is concerned. Reprinted many times, and read, I am sure, by many of those now reading this text, the essay was entitled, "The Human Situation: A Feminine View."[19] It is recognized by many women and men in theology and religious studies as a critical point of departure, since it framed many subsequent questions concerning what was implicit in women's (and men's) religious education, and talked of the implications continuing in the same way had for all human beings.

At the time she wrote it, Saiving was studying the ethical thought of Anders Nygren and Reinhold Niebuhr, especially their understanding and teaching about sin. At the same time she was reading Margaret Mead, and reflecting on her own experience and that of women generally. And the differences she was noticing prompted her to ask whether the idea of sin, defined as "pride" and "self-love" and "will to power" (as it had been defined for centuries), really described the sinfulness of women, or whether **our** sinfulness was not better suggested "by such items as triviality, distractibility and diffuseness; lack of an organizing center or focus; dependence on others for one's own self-definition; tolerance at the expense of standards of excellence; inability to respect the boundaries of privacy; sentimentality, gossipy sociability, and mistrust of reason—in short, underdevelopment or negation of the self."[20]

Saiving's question is critical in considering what is implicit in teaching, I believe, not so much because of the divergence in the understanding of sin it posits, but because of the deeper issue it raises of how our approaches to knowledge and understanding, teaching and learning are shaped by our assumptions, our presuppositions, and our being in the world—our experience of being men and our experience of being women. Her research reminds us as teachers that we need to look not only at what is taught, but at how it was decided what was to be taught—and at who decided. By extension, her research is a lament for the many losses to the entire human community, men as well as women, incurred by positing only one view as **the** view, whether that view is male, or female, or North American or white or even Christian. And her thought is a direct appreciation of the power of the implicit curriculum, which centers not so much on **what is taught** as it does on **the ways of approaching what is taught**, the choice of mentors and processes and intellectual frameworks to guide us as well as the questions it poses concerning *all* of the most fundamental meanings which interpret human life: not only sin, but love, friendship, justice, mercy, sexuality, religion, God.

But the silence is perhaps most profound and most deafening when we come to the Null Curriculum—to what is left out, both as content and as process. As we come to study **content**, we have begun to realize that we have left out much of the world in our study, that theology, for example, has been Western European or North American to the very recent past, and that theology being done elsewhere still tends to be labeled as "liberation" theology or "third world" theology, rather than as—simply—theology. Our study of the Judeo-Christian tradition, for example, has been overwhelmingly Christian, with the "Judeo" aspect ending at the first century, rather than being viewed as a great parallel faith, a stream accompanying our own into the present day. And although the voices of white, middle-class women are now being heard, the sound of the voices of women of color throughout the world still remains mute and unheard in almost everyone's education—including their own.[21]

When we come to study **process**, the other aspect of the null curriculum, and use that as a lens, we may begin to realize how much our teaching still relies on one-way instruction (teacher to student), and is directed toward grades, or toward getting into college, or passing college boards; how unchanged are our ways of going about the activity of teaching; how "set" is our geography in schools, with the board, and the desk, and sometimes the platform set in the front, and all seats arranged so that people do not engage—except with difficulty—with one another. And as we begin to address these circumstances and incorporate other procedures (we will return to this in Section 4, Artistry), we begin to acknowledge the need for more profound, deeper processes—processes beyond those of two-way communication, and physical change of rooms. These are processes which can lead to changes in the institutions where teaching goes on. These are processes drawn from the lives of women, such as those offered in this book.

For the Null Curriculum is faced when we begin by naming the Silences in our teaching and begin to address them; when we go on to all the different forms of Re-Membering which are then called for; when we find it valuable to take the time to Mourn our silent past, and when we then go on to the re-creative, and inventive work of Artistry, and the conviction that out of such themes and processes, Birth will eventually come. To get to that, however, the starting point will be our responding to the Silence.

RESPONSES TO SILENCE

When we recognize how few of our stories have been told, or, when they have been preserved, how little they have been attended to, a first and fitting response is sorrow and loss, as recorded in this reflection of Rosemary Cingari.

I have spent the past year speaking to teenagers, and using people from the Scriptures as real folks that they can grab hold of and embrace. Every time I bring up Miriam, the sister of Moses, who saved his life, without whom the Israelites would have had to look for another to lead them out of slavery, they have no clue as to who she is.

Yes, **is**, not **was**. Miriam holds great lessons for us. What does it mean to hold life as sacred? What does it mean to use creative problem solving to deal with the impossible? What does it mean to look for what you have in common with your greatest enemy to find life and salvation? Lessons we need. Lessons as great as the ones of her brother.

Miriam is part of my blood, my life, as alive for me as she was for Moses. I heard about Moses when I was five. I found Miriam when I was 30.[22]

Another response is alienation, a situation recorded by Carol Christ reflecting on the absence of women from biblical stories, where

. . . each woman engaged in the process of recovering her own experience will experience a deepened and deepening alienation from the traditional stories. We will no longer be content to read ourselves sidewise into stories in which 'the daughters do not exist.' We will find that self-identification with the sons and other male images and symbols in the language of the Bible and the tradition requires us to reject our particular identities as women—the very identities we are engaged in recovering and affirming in all the other important areas of our lives. [And] as our consciousness of the shapes and contours of our own experiences deepens, we will begin to realize that the exclusion of our experience from the funding of sacred stories may point to a basic defect in the perception of ultimate power and reality provided by the traditional stories.[23]

A further response, however, nourished by sorrow and loss, anger and alienation is to realize that these insights into silences—our own and others'—have awakened us, and that the possibility of an appropriate response lies within us and within our communities. And so the coming-to, the awakening to silence throughout the curriculum can bring us to the conviction that we—teachers and students—can address the theme of silence by refusing to be silent from now on. Perhaps by ourselves at first, we can begin to practice: practice saying our own names and finding our own voices. Beginning with not-too-threatening situations and then, nurtured by courage and community in more difficult ones, we can begin to speak up "carefully listening and responding in a conversation of free selves." And in doing so we can learn something about ourselves and about our own possibilities, capabilities and power. A character in Canadian novelist Margaret Atwood's *Surfacing* puts this response into words that have been revelatory for many women before us:

> This above all, to refuse to be a victim. Unless I can do that, I can do nothing. I have to recant, give up the old belief that I am powerless and because of it nothing I can do will ever hurt anyone. A lie which was always more disastrous than the truth would have been. The word games, the winning and losing games are finished; at the moment there are no others, but they will have to be invented; withdrawing is no longer possible and the alternative is death.[25]

Still another response, incumbent on teachers especially, but to be conveyed to students as a way of empowering one another is to learn to tune in to the silences, to wait for them, and then to address them, in ways already suggested by Adrienne Rich. "As women teachers," she tells us, "we can either deny the importance of this context in which women students think, write, read, study, project their own futures; or try to work with it. We can either teach passively, accepting these conditions, or actively, helping our students identify and resist them."[26] We can refuse to accept passivity, she tells us, in ourselves or in one another; we can give to one another the kind of cultural prodding men receive, but on different terms and in different styles.[27]

But as important as any response to the generative theme of silence is the use of silence itself: not as
a negative force, but as a positive one, as a healing
power. For this first generative theme of Silence is
multi-faceted, multi-layered, and richly textured. In
some instances, as we have seen, silence is a demon to
be exorcised. But at the same time, and from other
points of view, silence—notably contemplative silence,
the silence of compassionate listening—is a compan-
ion to be befriended. Silence before the mystery which
holds us and cherishes us can be the power healing the
wounds that other silences inflict. Powerful positive silence can lead to the discovery of the divinity within,
where, like poet/playwright Ntozake Shange, we find
god in ourselves and learn to love her, learn to love
her fiercely.[28] Contemplative silence can be the thematic universe where we discover ourselves made in
the image of this divinity, and able to use her wisdom,
her truth, her power as our own. If we would be wise
women attending to silence which destroys, we need
at the same time to be engaging the silence which cre-
ates and heals. We need to learn to recognize the presence of the One who so often comes clothed in silence,
as the Still Presence, and as the Awesome Shekinah,
who is ready to be our sister and our guide.

For Hers is the silence of listening and receptivity,
the silence of the old woman who knows the value in
the proverb, "Sometimes ah sets and waits, and sometimes ah jes sets." Hers is the silence where, while becoming receptive to others—our students, our

colleagues, our world—we also practice receptivity to ourselves. Surely it was such silence which was symbolized by Virginia Woolf, in wishing for women five hundred pounds a year and a room of one's own. For in Woolf's own words, the five hundred pounds symbolized the power to contemplate; the room of one's own symbolized the power to think for oneself—to receive oneself. To have a room of one's own, a quiet room, a soundproof room would allow women to hear silences, including their own, and, because of it, find a voice. But for such listening and the creative artistry it inspires, "there must be freedom and there must be peace. Not a wheel must grate, not a light glimmer. The curtains must be close drawn," so that the human being, in mind and spirit, "might celebrate its nuptials in darkness."[29] For in such healing darkness and stillness lie the conditions for a complete education.

And so in addition to the other responses we have named, a final and critical response for the teacher completing these first rhythmic moves in the step of Silence is to remember that all music has places of rest and that a spirituality of pedagogy must have room for prayerful silence. And in **this** music, at **this** step, the place of rest is care-filled listening, quiet reflection, abundant prayer, and deepened awareness. Attuned to these, the teacher and the learner can then move on, into the second step which issues out of Silence. Together they can be poised for the movement of Remembering.

2:
REMEMBERING

The turn from Silence to Remembering is a natural one, for out of the awareness and listening provoked by silence, and out of the sense of loss and alienation provoked by the null curriculum, previously unheard voices now make their claim. Sometimes the voices are our own; sometimes those of other people; sometimes those of earth. Sometimes the voice is of a previously unheard feminine divinity. In a spirituality of teaching, the work to which these voices call is that of going back and going down in order to re-call, reconnect and rediscover those who and that which has been forgotten, discarded or denied. But the work is also to become involved in processes and procedures which may be unfamiliar to us, or un-used as aspects of our learning and teaching. And so Remembering: a step which is *mythic*, which is *dangerous*, which is *communal*, which is *liturgical*. As we move through this step, we will consider each of these ways of remembering as well as its pedagogical implications.

Throughout all cultures, and for centuries, the great mythic figure has been the hero: the individual and separated self who at best is impregnable and impermeable, and who to prove himself often triumphs by slaying the monster. In our own time, however, this myth has become more and more brittle, as individual men and women question such an absolutist and anxiety-producing ideal. In its stead has come a reemergence of understanding not only of the hero, but of the mythic monster who till now has been kept at a distance.

It is instructive to find, as Catherine Keller points out, that the word **monster** stems from the root **mens**, out of which springs the entire family of memory words: **to remember, to remind, anamnesis, to commemorate**.[1] "The powerful images of mythic monsters disclose as irresistibly as dreams [our] displaced and denied possibilities,"[2] Keller tells us, suggesting that far from being foreign, strange or outsiders, monsters are projections of the parts of ourselves which are frightening because unfamiliar. And for cultures, they are the parts of the total society which are reminders of what has been left out: women's stories, for example, or thinking with our bodies, as well as our minds. Just as good teaching does, monsters remind us—show/demonstrate—of the complete picture. In remembering them, we re-member ourselves.

The mythic component of Remembering arises here through commemoration, one of the forms of remembering, which is always myth's ritual, enabling us to do the work of recalling and reconnecting with the great mythic figures. If we would reclaim and reintegate those figures, and more "if we wish no longer to participate in the heroic myth, which almost every institution in our civilization ritually reenacts daily, [in politics, big business, economics, military conflict, sport and entertainment] then we can only join in what the monster commemorates by commemorating the monster."[3]

Concretely, the pedagogical task thus becomes a remembering of the mythic, monstrous figures of the Medusa, the Goddess, the Hag and the Witch, a remembering which will help us face the monsters inside and outside ourselves, rather than blaming our mothers as we too often do, for our fears and our terrors. The mythic demand in remembering is the demand of facing our own pasts and our own presents, our own fears and our own shadows, discovering in doing so that the monster is after all not our enemy. Keller quotes a counsel of Alice Walker which is pertinent here: "Let us be intimate with/ancestral ghosts/and music/of the undead."[4] Keller also notes the power-filled quality of naming the deep memories of the monster as described by Mary Daly: "The rhythms of Naming deep Memory are . . . Tidal."[5]

We can grasp something of this Tidal power as we reencounter the Medusa. Originally gorgeous, and possessing lovely hair as the crown of her beauty, Medusa was raped by Poseidon, the Lord of the Sea. It was she, however, who was punished and the punishment was to have her hair turned into revolting serpents. Like so many women before and since, the victim is blamed, and the faces of those near her are averted, doubling her pain. No longer can they gaze at the serpents. But this **is** the work of mythic remembering: gazing at what originally terrifies, and turning it into a symbol of hope and new life. In this case, for example, if we gaze at the serpents long enough, we come to see they are the intertwined symbols in the caduceus, the sign of healing.

Eventually, Medusa is murdered, her head severed from her body by Perseus (what would the hero be if he did not have "monsters" to slay?) and she becomes, in a strange way, allied to the goddess Athena, born from the head of Zeus. Their alliance lies in their symbolizing a kind of existing which denies wholeness, denies the female body. For in both figures, Medusa and Athena, the heroic myth becomes fixed through the act of severing the head from the body, or, as in Athena's story, denying the need of any female body even for birth itself to occur. Only the head of the god is necessary. In their persons, then, they prefigure a way of learning and teaching that continues to survive today and which any spirituality of teaching must resist. This is a learning and teaching which separates head from body. Thus, the great task mythic remembering uncovers: a commitment to learning which occurs through the body as well as through the mind; to a learning which is artistic, aesthetic, fleshy and whole. In an environment where too much pedagogy still specializes in the work of separating heads from bodies, espcially in the presence of women of power, this will be our work.

The second move in this step will be to face the form of remembering taught to us most recently by John Baptist Metz, the political theologian. In *Faith in History and Society*, Metz instructs us in **dangerous** memory, writing that there are

> . . . memories which make demands on us. There are memories in which earlier experiences break through to the centre-point of our lives and reveal new and dangerous insights for the present. They illuminate for a few moments and with a harsh steady light the questionable nature of things we have apparently come to terms with, and show up the banality of our supposed 'realism'. They break through the canon of the prevailing structures of plausibility and have certain subversive features. Such memories are like dangerous and incalculable visitations from the past. They are memories that we have to take into account, memories, as it were, with a future content.[6]

In the lives and learning of women, the time for dangerous memory is now, especially in the two forms of memories of **suffering** and memories of **freedom**. Among the memories of suffering still to be incorporated into the mainstream of education, along with those of myth, are those of history, imagery and process. Mary Daly in *Gyn-Ecology*[7] and Andrea Dworkin in *Woman-Hating*[8] have illuminated much of the history of women's suffering, still absent from too many syllabi. They describe the major forms such suffering has taken throughout the centuries: from African genital mutilation, to Chinese foot-binding, to Hindu suttee (the burning of the widow upon the death of her husband), to the murder of over a million women in Europe as "witches" (with a published handbook to accompany the travesty), to the still-continuing practice of unnecessary removal of wombs and breasts in U.S. gynecological practice. Dworkin conveys something of the horror of one of these practices in the following paragraphs about real women and real little girls:

> Find a piece of cloth 10 feet long and 2 inches wide.
> Find a pair of children's shoes.
> Bend all toes except the big one under and into the sole of the foot. Wrap the cloth around these toes and then around the heel. Bring the heel and toes as close together as possible. Wrap the full length of the cloth as tightly as possible.
> Squeeze foot into children's shoes.
> Walk.
> Imagine that you are 5 years old.
> Imagine being like this for the rest of your life.[9]

I would argue that the failure to teach and to study such travesty (in contrast to our study of war, battle and conquest, even of popes and councils), especially in religious circles, is tied to our evasion of—our failure to remember—the image of the Christa. For although we have innumerable representations of the male crucified figure, there are very few images of the crucified as female. Australian painter Arthur Boyd is one of the artists who has faced this in his own work. Sculptor Edwina Sandys, whose four-foot bronze statue of a female crucified, called the "Christa," is another. But when her Christa was displayed during the 1980's in the United States, although much of the response was appreciative, much of it was rejecting. Some even thought it theologically "indefensible."[10] Apparently, although the obscenity of women's suffering can be silently tolerated, its artistic demonstration cannot—a challenge to any serious teacher of religious art.

This denial or paucity of imagery can have the direct result of keeping women from drawing life from the dangerous memory of suffering, from realizing that suffering can be redemptive. Dorothee Soelle has written that suffering has three phases, especially pertinent in the lives of women. The first is mute, passive acceptance, the suffering of the victim—Silence. The second is awareness and articulation of suffering—refusal to be a victim, risking the work of speaking out,—lamenting. And the third is organizing to change the conditions which produce suffering, a moment which can come only when change is seen as a value and possibility, and where dangerous memory has challenged the present situation.[11]

Another set of dangerous memories, however,

are the memories of freedom. In our own country, and against momentous odds, many women in education earlier in this century exercised such freedom, bringing us into the present and reminding us we stand on the shoulders of giants. Certainly Madeleva's stubborn persistence for years, advocating an NCEA teacher-preparation section, despite rejection, was the catalyst that brought the Sister Formation program into being, and with it the higher education of thousands of Catholic Sisters—a still uncalculated gift to the U.S. Catholic Church.[12] Certainly the courage of Mary Perkins Ryan, first in the liturgical movement, later in the work of family education, then in the questioning of forms of Catholic schooling, and most recently in the superb editorship of PACE, has been a fifty-year memory of a woman freely, but often over huge obstacles, exercising her gifts.[13] And certainly the contribution of Fannie Lou Hamer, a living embodiment and remembering of the teaching principles of black people, is a dangerous memory with a future content. A poor, Mississippi sharecropper with little formal schooling, Fannie Lou Hamer became an outstanding voice for other poor people denied their rights by racist social structures. Despite assault, jailing, threat and opposition, her work for justice won victory for her people.[14] All of us, but especially women, need these memories of freedom in our educations.

We also need to celebrate the dangerous memories of women who work for peace: Molly Rush, mother of six and grandmother of two who has given us in her own demonstrating and imprisonment a mantra for any spirituality: "What about the children?"[15] The mothers and grandmothers of the Plaza de Mayo in Buenos Aires, walking silently for years, as they processed in a circle and held the pictures of children and grandchildren—**desaparecidos**—as a defiant challenge to a repressive government.[16] And the women of Greenham Common, sitting even now in bitter cold and driving rain around a fire, ready to greet all visitors, and in their own persons dangerous memories of freedom and hospitality and healing to the world—women who leave other symbols behind to teach us their ways:

> Anyone looking at the Greenham fence would have been struck by the way the might of the weapons was opposed by the most fragile things: personal possessions, baby clothes, wool. Someone left an egg in the mesh of the fence, inscribed 'For peace'. Aggression was met not by closing oneself in, armouring oneself, but by exposing one's vulnerability, by making visible what the dominating power excludes or denies. This turns what are supposed to be signs of weakness into symbols of strength.[17]

And into dangerous memories.

COMMUNAL REMEMBERING

Remembering is an incomplete step, however, if the only voices, the only lives, the only silences we

39

commemorate are those of women. In fact, one test of the genuineness of our care for an appropriate spirituality of teaching will be our remembering other unheard voices: those silenced because of race, sexual orientation, economic hardship or political choices; the silences of men, bruised as women are, by structures and systems which fail to liberate. For just as a belief in the Mystical Body or the Communion of Saints teaches us that if one suffers, all suffer, so too belief in the communal element of remembering will illuminate the truth that if any are forgotten, all are penalized.[18]

Therefore, the communal element in Remembering will also need to be a step in our teaching. Here Remembering as a pedagogical task will be directed to the unrepresented and the underrepresented in our teaching. At one level, this would mean our monitoring our work to examine whether all our sources, all our authorities are Western European or North American—or, especially in religion or theology, all male clergymen, or whether we also include the Asian world, the African world, the Australian world, and the Americas south of the U.S. border, in addition to including women and unordained men. At another level, it will mean our monitoring our work to examine whether, in addition to the successes and the joys of our traditions, we also give attention to the failures and the sorrows. In Christian educational circles, for example, we have yet to re-member in any integrated way that great fissure of evil crossing the twentieth century, the destruction of European Jewry—more specifically, the Christian preparation for, participation in, and responsibility toward our Jewish brothers and sisters—before the holocaust and since.[19] And in political life, when stories of torture and exile and denial of civil rights are reported to us, we need to remember a message smuggled out of a Philippine prison during the Marcos regime: "If you want to really understand us, listen closely to what we are not allowed to say."[20]

Inevitably, communal Remembering should impel us to incorporate into our teaching not only other human beings, but the earth itself, and to imagine as we educate what relation our work has to the entire non-human universe: land, water, fire, air, as well as the other animals with whom we share the planet.[21] Such remembering will be sacramental in that it respects the teaching power in all creation: of oil, incense, wax; of animals toward humans; of a cactus, a hurricane, a wren, a thornbush. An exercise I use which brings this home is the following which can be done with one, or fifty, or a hundred people in a room:

1. Choose an object such as a stone, leaf, blade of grass, stick or other outside object.
2. Sit quietly with your object.
3. Ask the object about itself, its story, its history. Where has it been ... who has touched it, held it, walked past it without noticing?
4. Where was it born? How did it get there?

   Sit quietly and wait for the answers.

41

5. Then ask the object about its inner life, its spirituality. Ask about its vulnerability, its tenderness, its destiny, its relations with others.

    Sit quietly and wait for the answers; listen when they come.

6. What does it wish to tell you? What does it say about your intuitions? Your questions? Your depths?

7. And finally what if anything does the object tell you of God?[22]

This exercise is an attempt to give flesh to the teaching found in the eighth chapter of the Epistle to the Romans, Paul's insight that, along with humanity, the entire creation is in travail, groaning and aching to see if the human community will extend beyond itself to include the community of the rest of creation.[23] Communal Remembering is the step in teaching leading to that inclusion.

LITURGICAL REMEMBERING

The last aspect in the step of Remembering is **an-amnesis**, that form of memory which is especially linked with the Eucharist, but which is essential to all genuine teaching. **Anamnesis** is a *recalling to mind* (its literal translation) as is all remembering. However, it is not so much a mental act as it is the actual bringing into the present—the **re-membering**—of a past event through ceremonial representation or liturgy. At the core of anamnesis is the human capacity to take hold of an event or occurrence or person from the historical past **in the present**, and to allow that event, occurrence or person to take hold of oneself. The distinguishing character of Jewish and Christian anamnesis is that although the past remains in force as past, and as accomplished, human beings are able to reactualize the past in their own time and in their own present lives beyond merely intellectual recall. Anamnesis—or liturgical remembering—is always a human possibility, because human beings are permanently established within the universe.[24] And the unity of history, and herstory, means that those lives which we have already lived retain their validity and remain historically established.

Such anamnesis applies especially to the Christ, in the traditions of Catholicism and Orthodoxy. But by extension, because all are "in Christ" as other aspects of the Imago Dei, we may say that anamnesis is an aspect of all teaching, especially if we believe the teaching act is a religious act. As such, it becomes a further ritual of Remembering where as teachers and learners we reenter the past and make it our own; we re-view the lives of others and incorporate them into ours; we rediscover unspoken words and allow them to speak to us.

Doing that demands the creation of ceremonies of our own which are based on Re-Membering so that the past may take hold of us even as we take hold of it. We have already noted the power of commemoration in speaking of Mythical Remembering; here we

43

go one step further and incorporate into our teaching actual rituals of commemoration.

To assist us in doing this, many women and groups of women are publishing records of readings, rituals and ceremonies which engage in liturgical re-membering. Linda Clark, Marian Ronan and Eleanor Walker were among the first in their collection, *Image-Breaking, Image Building*,[25] and have been followed by others such as Janet Kalven and Mary Buckley et al. in *Women's Spirit Bonding*,[26] Rosemary Ruether's *WomanGuides*,[27] Diane Mariechild's *Mother Wit*[28] and the ongoing work of W.A.T.E.R—the Woman's Alliance for Theology, Ethics and Ritual in Silver Spring, Maryland.[29] Among the most powerful ceremonies of liturgical remembering in which I have participated are those built on Judy Chicago's art work, *The Dinner Party*, where all the women present designed place-mats commemorating forgotten women.[30] Following that, at an agreed-upon moment, we toasted the memories and the lives of those we were re-membering. I have taken part in toasts to Mary and Elizabeth, Eve and Lilith, Medea and Anne Frank. And in doing so, I, like the women whose company I shared, ceremonially reappropriated a past which until then had not been fully mine.

Those moments, however, were not without pain, and not without tears. Nor are the moments of communal, dangerous and mythic remembering. For in the remembering there is weeping and there is loss; there is grieving and there is sorrow; there is anger and often there is rage. And the steps in the dance now pause as the memory of the loss is faced and the next step emerges. Having Remembered, we now re-alize we must permit ourselves an even deeper ritual. We have come to the step of Mourning.

3:
RITUAL MOURNING

One dynamic in the step of Remembering is the inner urge we feel toward movement: toward processes and procedures for confronting the situation we have been studying in order to change it. "It is better to light one candle than to curse the darkness," we say; or "Don't just stand there; do something." But a deeper dynamic in the step of Remembering is toward another **kind** of process and procedure where we **do** pause to curse the darkness; where we momentarily **do** stand still, in acknowledgement and understanding, and where we realize that before we take the next step, toward artistry, we need to pause and go down into the depths, in order to face the feelings and the awarenesses brought forth by memory. This pause—a slow movement in the dance—is the step that follows Remembering: Ritual Mourning.

A year ago, while I was giving a workshop on Women and Justice in Oregon, a participant approached me at the midway point. "I don't think I can continue," she said, "because I'm so deeply troubled and feel such pain at what we're talking about here. My anger, my rage, my feelings are all at the surface." Her experience of bringing to the surface what had been hidden a long time is familiar to most women as one of the reasons for mourning; and she and I spoke there and then as one of its rituals. Familiar too is the refrain from Judy Collins' "Bread and Roses" where the singers recall that as women today "go marching, marching, unnumbered women dead go crying through our singing their ancient call for bread."[1] Our ritual mourning, commemorating them, is allowing their voices to speak once more. And both—the Oregon woman and the singers—are points of departure for the step of Ritual Mourning, where we pause to examine (a) what mourning is, (b) the forms of mourning, (c) why we mourn, and (d) how we mourn.

What Mourning Is

Mourning is the generative theme which provides the necessary passageway between remembering and artistry. John Keats described it as

Most like the struggle at the gate of death
Or liker still to one who should take leave of
    pale, immortal death
And with a pang as hot as death is chill
With fierce convulse, die into life.[2]

In education, mourning is the step where teachers and learners are called to die into life. For if we grant that education is to remember and out of that remembering to recreate new forms; if we believe that teaching is the work of taking seriously the experience of all of

47

us and being critical of how and when it does or does not; and if we believe we must develop a pedagogy which incorporates the fullness of women's lives; then much of our present limited concentration on only a part of human history, and many of the procedures presently included and excluded, will have to be examined. Much if not most will have to be discarded. Massive change will be required. And out of such work will come the taking leave "of pale, immortal death," and the birth of something new. And the best name to give to this time of passage is mourning: going down into the forgotten underworlds within and outside ourselves and facing the loss, bereavement and grief occasioned by such a journey.

In 1942, a tragic fire swept a Boston night club called the Cocoanut Grove. Within thirty minutes, 492 people were dead. After the occurrence, Erich Lindemann interviewed survivors and bereaved, and gave us one of the first technical descriptions of what is involved in grieving and mourning. Six characteristics were especially evident: (1) somatic, bodily distress; (2) intense preoccupation with the image of who/what was lost; (3) guilt; (4) a disconcerting lack of warmth; (5) disorganized patterns of conduct; (6) the feeling you no longer fit.[3] I find a remarkable degree of correspondence in the presence of these characteristics not only in the bereaved of that tragedy, but in women today beginning to face our pasts. In such circumstances, the work of learning is itself often disorganized, painful, sorrow-filled and touched by loss.

Elisabeth Kübler-Ross continued research into mourning and grief and elaborated five stages, applicable to the terminally ill, but also descriptive of those who mourn them: denial, anger, bargaining, depression and acceptance.[4] The woman in Oregon, for example, spoke with me out of her depression, her anger and her past denial; the singing women in "Bread and Roses" are incorporating theirs into a grieving remembrance at the same time they say "No, never, never again." And those of us striving to create a spirituality of teaching are learning to deal with our anger and our rage.

As elements in mourning, rage and anger are particularly pertinent to women and pedagogy. Often the first sign of new awareness comes when a woman realizes how much of her communal past and her personal capabilities have been lost to her or left unaddressed in her education, and expresses that anger in the academic setting. (I can still remember the first of my own woman students doing that, in Madison, New Jersey, and the way she helped me in facing my own denial, my own anger, my own grieving.) Perhaps no one has written about the importance of such anger as eloquently as Beverly Harrison in noting the miseducation caused in Christianity by calling anger a deadly sin. In contrast, writes Harrison, anger is **not** a human failure.

> It is better understood as a feeling-signal that all is not well in our relation to other persons or groups or to the world around us. Anger is a **mode of connectedness** to others and it is always a **vivid form of caring**. To put the point another way: anger is—and it **always**

is—a sign of some resistance in ourselves to the moral quality of the social relations in which we are immersed. Extreme and intense anger signals a deep reaction to the action upon us or toward others to whom we are related.[5]

And Harrison concludes, "To grasp this point . . . is a critical first step in understanding the power of anger in the work of love."[6] What I would add is that to grasp this point is also to realize that the anger of many of our students, women and men, is also a critical first step in the process of mourning, as they confront the moral quality of their educational social relations.

THE FORMS OF MOURNING

If mourning is healthy and complete it will take at least three forms: it will be personal, communal and societal. Although it usually begins with our own experience of loss or with how we have been affected by loss in our educations, it will have a natural impetus out to other women and then toward the wider society. In fact, one of the great dangers in engaging in only one form of mourning (the personal) is that it can turn inward, lead us to continue portraying ourselves as victims if we are already doing so, and keep us stuck in a pattern of denial. Thus, all three forms are necessary.

The first form of mourning, however, is generally at a *personal* level. "Metaphorically, a psychological death occurs whenever we are forced to let go of something or someone and must grieve for the loss. The death may be an aspect of ourselves, an old role, a former position, or beauty or other youthful qualities that are now gone and must be mourned, or a dream that is no more. Or it may be a relationship, ended by death or distance, that leaves us grieving."[7] Carolyn Osiek describes this form in *Beyond Anger*, giving particular attention to the loss occurring from broken symbol systems, where all the religious paraphernalia of a patriarchal world becomes as dust in the mouth, and to the time of **impasse**, where there is no resolution found in dodging or denying pain, and where the more one tries to escape, the worse things get. Here, the only way out is through.[8] Yet at some moment the way out does appear, and often is because of an awareness that we are not alone in our suffering and that our feelings resonate with those of others.

Communal mourning then becomes allied to this first form. And here we recognize that the experience of loss is shared, especially with other women, and move to begin the work of communion and bonding with one another. Theologian Edwina Hunter, one of those who **did** acknowledge the power of the Christa when it was exhibited, gives voice to the nature of this kind of mourning:

> No sermon in words I have ever heard preached has moved me to such oneness with all my crucified sisters everywhere— whatever their color, race, nationality, or

51

economic standing. The Christa does for us what no statue of a crucified ethnic male can do: it breaks down ethnic barriers, cuts across all lines, expresses all woman-humanity in our nakedness, vulnerability, and death. And it is exactly at this point that the Christa becomes fully a sermon of hope, because it is as we embrace our own nakedness and vulnerability and death [as we mourn] that we find we can also embrace the tomb.[9]

Yet, in order to be complete, communal mourning is not only individual or conceptual recognition and acknowledgement; it is embodied in concrete, shared expression. One way this was done recently was through the report of the "Women in Pain Working Group" which was part of the 1982 Women's Spirit Bonding Conference at Grailville Ohio.[10] That group, in addition to reflecting together, produced a litany of women in pain, where communally the group acknowledged:

> I am the voice of the woman who has been beaten, threatened and abused. . . .
> I speak for the elderly woman. I feel our society wants to throw me away. . . .
> I speak for the battered children, for the victims of incest and rape. . . .
> I speak for the one who was too shy to be heard. . . . [11]

A third form of communal mourning comes when we are strong enough to face our differences. The racially diverse group of women in religion who co-authored *God's Fierce Whimsy*, for example, has the courage to name, acknowledge and talk about their differences, especially along racial lines, and in doing so provide a model for women striving to overcome those and other divisions such as nationality, politics or poverty/wealth. To read of their engagement with one another and be allowed into their struggle is to take part in an embodiment of communal mourning.[12]

Through ways such as these, personal and communal mourning then open and embrace a third form, *societal* mourning, where women acknowledge a cosmic grief over the entire human condition—the suffering touching any woman, any child, any man anywhere, as well as the cosmic suffering of the planet itself. It has a necessary component of rebellion, too, for

> . . . suffering is seen as a collective experience—as the experience of everyone . . . and the entire human race suffers from the division between itself and the rest of the world. The unhappiness experienced by a single man or woman becomes collective unhappiness. In our daily trials, rebellion plays the same role as does the 'cognito' in the category of thought: It is the first clue. But this clue lures the individual from his or her solitude. Rebellion is the **common** ground on which every human being bases his or her first values. **I rebel—therefore we exist.**[13]

This is participation in the prophetic mourning Abraham Heschel calls the divine pathos, and through it we meet the mourning of God.[14] At the step of Remembering we noted the movement toward **commemorating** all the silenced of the earth. Here we renew that movement, by adding societal and divine mourning to the personal and the communal. We acknowledge the presence of a Divine Pity. And the particular pertinence this has to developing a spirituality of teaching is that such mourning, begun out of the grieving of and for ourselves and other women, signals at its core a spirituality of justice.

Why We Mourn

Justice is at the core because all the forms of mourning—personal, communal and societal—are forms of grieving over the absence of justice. Rather than being based on a spirituality of passive acceptance, or of private endurance, they emerge out of an outrage against the injustice suffered by women, by the men who do not measure up to patriarchy, by the poor of the earth, and by the earth itself. For if it is true that justice is the structured struggle to share the goods of God's great earth,[15] and if justice is finding out what belongs to whom and giving it back,[16] then we must acknowledge we grieve as women because justice has not been ours; we grieve as human beings because justice still waits to be born.

We grieve in acknowledgement, and we grieve to acknowledge. As were our parents in the first garden, we too are commissioned to name, and in our grieving compelled to speak names never before said aloud, or spoken only in whispers. Indeed, if there is any answer at the heart of the question, "Why mourn?" it is this: the failure to pause, to acknowledge and to name is a desecration of memory. The hurry to do our own work, without pausing to notice the holiness of theirs, is to violate them. The absence of care toward those who are sedimented in our flesh and blood, living on in us, is to invite death of the spirit. And so we name our mothers, our grandmothers, our foremothers. We name our sisters, our daughters, our wives. We name our lovers and our friends. We name women of ideas, and women of bondage. We name bruised women, broken women, slave women. We name brilliant women, artistic women, literary women. We name women become numbers in the hells of Auschwitz and Bergen-Belsen, and women become castaways on the streets of New York. We hold our own Dinner Party. And in doing so we begin leaning into the work of artistry.

But we also mourn to express our feelings. The awareness of the absence of women and women's voices, the awakening to the null curriculum in our educations, causes the most intense and severest feelings of loss that many students have ever known, and so into the teaching situation, and into spirituality itself, comes the celebration of feeling: feelings of anger, denial, guilt, bereavement and loneliness. And once again, it is anger which is revelatory, this time of a deeper reality, love.

Anger directly expressed is a mode of taking the other seriously, of caring. The important point is that where feeling is evaded, where anger is hidden or goes unattended, masking itself, there the power of love, the power to act, to deepen relation, atrophies and dies. . . . We can ignore, avoid, condemn or blame. Or, we can act to alter relationship toward reciprocity, beginning a real process of hearing and speaking to each other.[17]

Which is the final reason we mourn, and especially why we mourn together: for many women it is the beginning of speech. Shared mourning and shared feeling erupt into spoken, articulated patterns. And if we are developing a spirituality of teaching, feeling expressed verbally in an educational setting need never be reversion to **sheer** feeling, or to feeling alone. Instead it can be the opportunity for speaking which is **whole** and therefore for **whole** learning, the wedding of feeling with thought. "The task is clear, although the solution is not."[18] Indeed, poet Marge Piercy could have been giving us one last answer to the question "Why mourn" in very simple words. The reason we mourn is that it brings us to the moment of "Unlearning to not speak."[19]

How We Mourn

The name of this step is not mourning alone; it is Ritual Mourning. And the reasons are, I believe, clear;

mourning is healing, and educational, and the basis of a spirituality if it is done in community and in communion with one another. Done alone, there is too much danger that mourning will turn us in on ourselves, and not lead us on to the next step. For this reason, the step needs to be attentive to those forms through which we can grieve together, in formal and structured ways. Perhaps even more than Re-Membering, this step demands rituals.

"In its deepest, most spiritual sense," writes Francine du Plessix Gray, "ritual is a sequence of gestures that repeats a primordial act, such as the Christian rite of communion which symbolizes our sisterhood and brotherhood in sharing the body of the Godhead, or the rite of Passover which symbolizes the miraculous survival of the Jewish people."[20] Therefore it should come as no surprise that rituals of mourning today draw on such acts as breaking bread and passing the cup, as in Christian liturgy, as well as in recalling the ten plagues fallen upon women, as described by Letty Cottin Pogrebin as part of a woman's Seder: "the plague of being an unwanted daughter, or taken for granted, of voices silenced and minds unused, of the rape, battery, and sexual exploitation, unacknowledged in the Jewish community; of defamation; and subordination; and lost dreams."[21] It should also come as no surprise that one of the earliest ritualistic women in legend, Antigone, committed civil disobedience by insisting on rites of mourning for her brother. In her insistence, as *necessary* before moving on, she can be a model for us, if not in the forms chosen, at least in her person.

Our own forms of mourning will have to fit our own situations. They can be verbal: spoken or sung. They can be totally without words: as simple as sitting in a circle in stillness or holding each other's hands; as complex as the Grand Right and Left, a metaphorical dance throughout the country performed in 1987–88 by the U.S. Sisters of Mercy.[22] With reference to the spoken, we might imitate Regina Coll of the University of Notre Dame, moving around a circle and asking women to complete such phrases as "I remember . . . ; I am saddened by . . . ; or "The thing I miss most from the past is . . . "[23] With reference to the sung, we might imitate Cris Williamson singing "Lean on me, I am your sister; believe in me, I am your friend,"[24] imagining as we do who is singing to whom. Or we might begin and end sessions inspired by Holly Near and Ronnie Gilbert in ways which overcome divisions: "We are young and old together; and we are singing, singing for our lives. We are gay and straight together; and we are singing, singing for our lives."[25] And as example of a silent ritual, we might pass a goblet of milk from one to the next, in commemoration of the female life in our bodies and our breasts.

But what rituals of mourning need not be is sad or solemn. Indeed, beyond song and silence, they can go on to include laughter and dance. Anyone who has ever been to an Irish wake knows that. But so too do all persons come together to acknowledge a life and accept its passing. The grieving is real; the loss is real; the pain is real. But the power of the ritual lies in its capacity to name the pain, face it, surface it, and then grant it burial. In doing that, ritual brings the step of mourning to completion and resolution, and prepares the way for imagination and creative power to appear on the stage. For Ritual Mourning now leads us into Artistry.

4:
ARTISTRY

One of the themes which has acted as an undersong throughout this essay is women's search to find a voice. We began tracing this theme by examining silence, noted unheard voices when we turned to remembering, and argued that one of the major reasons for Ritual Mourning is that it issues in "unlearning to not speak." As we turn now to Artistry, the step where we examine processes and procedures for women and pedagogy, we begin once again by reflecting on speech, this time from the perspectives of creativity and imagination.

In *Women's Ways of Knowing,* the authors write that women show a tendency to base their assumptions about knowing in metaphors more connected to speaking and listening than to those dealing with seeing, or with truth as "light."[1] Their research indicates to them, as it did in related work of physicist Evelyn Keller, that whereas images of vision and the mind's eye suggest standing at a distance in order to get a proper view, metaphors of hearing connote the characteristically female modes of closeness between subject and object, dialogue, interaction and connection.[2] These are our "natural" forms.

For this reason, although the term "imagination" is one which I have used extensively in my own work, I want to acknowledge that it **can** limit creative activity—or overstress only its visual possibilities. This is because it emphasizes, at least etymologically, such powers as imaging, imagining, and envisioning. In contrast, the theme of *Artistry* is a wider term which obviously has meaning for all the senses.[3] Not only does artistry assume hearing and sound as in music and dance, it also celebrates touch, as in sculpture and pottery and molding; place and geography as in architecture; the visual powers needed for painting and the graphic arts; the powers of voice and word needed for poetry, drama and literature; and the entire range of bodily capacities which lead to the "creation of form, expressive of human feeling" which Susanne Langer teaches **is** the work of art.[4]

The pertinence of this meaning of art is that, having moved through the first three steps, we turn now to the work of shaping those forms demanded by a pedagogy which takes women students seriously. We **could** choose to work as technicians or scientists or politicians or theologians—and as teachers we shall have to work in precisely these ways on many occasions. But if we are about the creation of something new, a far richer starting point, in my view, is to understand ourselves working as artists: bringing all of our senses to bear on the making of these forms; bringing all of the possibilities of art into conversation with each other; and believing that creating a spirituality of teaching is itself a work of art. That in turn will mean that we will be guided by questions of beauty

61

and wholeness, be ready to move where the material takes us, and will not allow ourselves to say, "Now it is finished. Nothing more needs to be done." Instead, like Starhawk, we will regularly move away from what is pre-formed and pre-written toward "ways of evoking spontaneity and creativity from those who come."[5] In what follows, therefore, I will try to model such artistry as a process for shaping pedagogy by attending to the rhythms of *Embodiment, Revelation, Receptivity to Power* and *Release*.[6]

EMBODIMENT

If art is the creation of form, then the first work of artist-teachers is the search for appropriate forms which will embody subject-matter. Embodiment, as the word suggests, means shaping, forming, giving flesh to and giving body to that which is to be taught. How to do this is one of the central questions still facing women and pedagogy, and although there is substantial creative discussion on academic content today, much less exists on **how** we teach. Writing from the women's Theological Center in Boston, for example, Pui Lan Kwok notes that one of the key issues in women's religious education continues to be that "the insights and visions of feminist theology do not find **embodiment** in the institutional structure of our schools."[7] In contrast, she writes,

> The WTC is committed to search for a pedagogy that integrates (a) content and pro-

cess, (b) intellect and emotion, (c) theory and practice. While the goals are clear, how to go about them is fraught with difficulties. We value the experiences of the participants, but we also do not want to stop only at the personal experience level without learning some tools or theories to analyse or integrate our own experiences. There is always tension in this. A lot of the tension comes from the strong reaction of some . . . such that they tend to view any disciplined study and analysis as a "male model" of learning; others become frustrated with what one student described as 'emotional bathos, that depresses without enlightening.' We are still searching for a process that can integrate the academic and experiential, our passions and emotions.[8]

In my view, Kwok is right in illuminating the value of critical thought, disciplined study, and theoretical analysis: these need not be carried out according to a male model. And she does name two forms of embodiment which **have** been integrated into the pedagogy of the WTC: field experience to test theory, and continuing and intense struggle with class, race and sexual biases among the participants themselves.[9]

The single most valuable resource I have come across to date which addresses women and teaching is Margo Culley and Catherine Portuges' edited collection *Gendered Subjects*.[10] The text describes numerous forms for embodying subject matter, centering on the teaching of women's studies. The authors are women and men, people of color, not all U.S., working in situations as diverse as Ivy League colleges and the downtown Detroit Y.W.C.A. The commitment and creativity demonstrated in facing the issues raised in this book is extraordinary, and the examples of ongoing work are exhilarating. To cite only two examples, one author writes of arriving one evening to a team-taught class (the team: one man, one woman) and changing the assignment.

> On the spot we asked each person to pair off with a partner and to take turns telling the stories of their mothers' lives. Our intention was simply to focus on generational differences and to introduce some historical consciousness but the exercise took much longer than we anticipated and clearly generated a high level of energy. When we returned to the group as a whole, our students insisted on sharing not their sense of history, but their excitement over unsuspected strengths they discerned in their mothers' life-stories.[11]

Silence. Remembering. Mourning—then delight. Artistry. Birth.

The other example comes from Michele Russell, detailing seven methodological principles as critical in teaching—principles which are characterized by poetry, creativity and artistry, which she has learned in teaching black women. As she names them,

1. Take one subject at a time.
2. Encourage story-telling.
3. Give political value to daily life.
4. Be able to speak in tongues.
5. Use everything.
6. Be concrete.
7. Have a dream.[12]

Other suggestions for embodying subject matter in ways which are true to women's lives come from those working with young women of high school age. The Feminist Press has published a high school women's studies curriculum called *Changing Learning, Changing Lives,* which draws on many alternative practices in teaching, beyond lecture-discussion, and has the added advantage of being adaptable for male-female groups too.[13] And Judith Dorney has developed a high school curriculum in religious education which asks the participants to draw and critique images of God; to listen to popular songs and read contemporary poetry for portraits of women; to explore understandings of society and world through simulation-game survival strategies; and to complete the curriculum by critiquing ourselves as teachers, since those attitudes we have learned through time and institutions die hard. As such she models a women's pedagogy at the same time she keeps analysis sharp.[14]

Similarly, Regina Coll draws on feminism to describe the Peaceable Classroom, eschewing competition as a learned behavior which reinforces the lesson that life is about beating other people. She proposes:

If students learn to work together in groups; if they learn from one another (not merely a bright student tutoring a slower one); if students' groups prepare projects and panels for the benefit of the whole class and not in order to compete for the best grades; if students take team tests working together toward a team grade, then perhaps they will learn that cooperation rather than competition is a viable way of learning and of living.[15]

Other suggestions for embodying subject matter come from Nancy Schniedewind, writing on "Guidelines for Teaching Methodology in Women's Studies," guidelines appropriate for all other disciplines. Among those she notes as crucial: development of an atmosphere of mutual respect, trust and community in the classroom; shared leadership—with students as well as other faculty; cooperative structures such as small group joint assignments to produce books, films, projects; the integration of cognitive and affective learning; and, as with the WTC noted above, action.[16]

And Gerda Lerner, in *Teaching Women's History*, offers a set of questions which, although directed to that discipline, are applicable to most others. Initiating students into learning how to think about women, she offers teaching questions designed to bring women into view:

1. Where and who are the missing women?
2. What did women do while the men were

doing what the textbook tells us was important?

3. How did women live? What did they do?
4. What did women contribute to abolition, to reform, to the labor movement? (Religion teachers might substitute their own categories here, such as spirituality, theology, morality.)
5. How did women define the issue?[17]

Such questions and activities are of course only examples. Yet if shaped with care, they are the kind which can lead to Revelation.

REVELATION

To bring the theme of Revelation into the act of teaching is both religious and educational.[18] From the religious perspective it suggests that all activity, including teaching and learning—perhaps especially these, since revelation is a form of knowing—offers opportunities for human beings to encounter the divine. From the educational perspective, however, it is even more a discovery that some forms of teaching and learning can lead to the revelation of oneself, in large part because they are more artistically designed. For if a subject is embodied in ways such as those suggested above, which take the wholeness and mystery of the human being seriously, then at some point the major meaning of subject matter becomes manifest and the hidden texture of "subject" is encountered as personal. For

> ... the term 'subject-matter' disguises an equivocation. It conflates two related but distinct meanings. On the one hand any subject-matter is a system of clues, concerned with human existence, organized about some initiating and defining concept, expressed in language and argued by human beings. On the other hand, subject matter is that world of meaning, order of nature, physical process, pattern of events, organization of feelings which the former kind of subject matter enables us to conceive. It is that labyrinth of reality through which and towards the understanding of which any particular discourse is a directing and guiding thread.[19]

Yet even that statement does not go deep enough. For a creative, artistic dynamic exists in subject matter, in the two senses just described, which pushes us to realize that the "labyrinth of reality" is pointing even more deeply toward *us*: to the human beings who are ourselves subjects, even more, subjects who *matter* in the sense Paulo Freire teaches.[20] Indeed, the human existence so dreamed of and demanded by women today arises from our conviction that authentic human existence and authentic human freedom assumes we are subjects. It arises from the demand that our teachers as well as we ourselves take us seriously as such **subjects** and as creators and artists who have **the on-**

68

tological vocation to **be** Subjects.[21] When **that** revelation comes, we have learned who and what is the genuine subject in all education.

And to facilitate such revelation, all of the embodiments mentioned above can help. But so too can an artistic process called indirect communication brought to bear on teaching—a way of working where a teacher's main purpose is not to deliver content to receivers of that content, but *to deliver human beings to themselves.*[22] In fact I believe that Revelation occurring in the context of teaching is precisely this: self-discovery; self-understanding; self-possession in a community of free and authentic selves. Revelation is the realization of deliverance: **by** the Mystery of God, but **of** ourselves **to** ourselves in communion with all that is.

The indirect communication which brings this about can never be forced, and this is why it is essentially artistic. But the **forms** of indirect communication, where suggestion and subtlety reign over imposition, can be named: masks, irony, asides, humor, digressions, paradox, parable, wit, expressive language over steno-language,[23] all the ways of art, and finally, the posing of questions that lead us to realize that in our own persons **we** are the essential questions that life presents. To paraphrase theologian Karl Rahner, human being is that being in whom Being is always in question. Or in the more poetic language of a character in *The Color Purple:*

> I think us here to wonder, to ast. And that in
> wondering 'bout the big things and asting

69

'bout the big things, you learn about the little ones, almost by accident. But you never know nothing more about the big things than you start out with. The more I wonder, he say, the more I love.[24]

Wondering. Asking questions. Posing questions of others. Critical questions. Analytical questions. Problem-posing questions as distinct from "guess what I'm thinking questions."[25] Questions such as "Who says?" "On what grounds?" "What are the benefits of that view?" "What are the limitations?" "Could this be different?" "How?" Genuine questions where the answers are unknown, discovered only in the questioning. All of these are actually characteristic of women, who pose questions more than men, and even more so of women who are mothers.[26] Indeed, Belenky et al. argue that the posing of questions is at the heart of the knowing which they call "connected," at the heart of knowing which is whole.[27] In a spirituality of teaching which leads to revelation, the pedagogical route may well be not only analyzing and pursuing such questions but living them too. For we need to

. . . be patient towards all that is unsolved . . . and try to love the questions themselves like locked rooms . . . not seek the answers; that cannot be given because you would not be able to live them. And the point is, to live everything. Live the questions now. Perhaps you will then gradually, without noticing it, live along some distant day into the answer.[28]

Once we take into ourselves the revelation of ourselves as subjects, a further dynamic appears. It is the realization that we have capacities and abilities, or, to use the word for capacity and ability, we have **power**. Delivered to ourselves, we realize we are existing, responsible, moral and religious **agents**, and not passive receivers. We are able to make choices, to initiate actions, to respond to demands. This, however, can be a troubling and painful discovery, a revelation we may be reluctant to accept.

For power is a word that elicits many and varied emotional reactions. For some people, power is a dirty word. They feel we demean and soil ourselves by having anything to do with it. For a teacher to say this appears to me disingenuous at best and scandalous at worst, for all teaching is an exercise of power. My own belief is that the emotional responses come not from power itself, but from the way it is understood and the way it is exercised. Too often, power is equated with force, violence and domination, and such meanings have of course been destructive to women. Yet for women, the past indicates that it is not genuine power which corrupts, but powerlessness—which, if it does not corrupt, still effectively keeps people from being subjects. Powerlessness can be especially power**ful**, in actuality, especially when it is preached as a way of keeping people (again, especially women) in their places. Still, because power is such a central reality in pedagogy, we must address it and examine what it might mean in our own lives.

In my teaching, after acknowledging the complexities of the word power, I generally propose that power is basically **capacity** and **ability**. Refining it further, I propose that it is the capacity and ability to **act**, but to act in two ways: as agent, doer, creator, shaper and designer; and as receiver, listener, hearer, responder, learner. This understanding draws on the knowledge that not only are all of us **acting** subjects, we are also always **responding** subjects—subjects who listen and who hear, and who out of that become **moral** subjects too, engaged in response-ability.[29] Further it emphasizes that all genuine teaching is directed to help learners come to this place of power. Jesse Jackson embodies this insight as he goes from school to school in the United States teaching young black people to shout out loud: "I am SomeBody!"

For many people, especially women, the dawning knowledge of capacities to act receptively or actively can be very frightening, especially if they have known only powerlessness. Such "unlearning" can attract and repel at the same time. Therefore, a teacher can be a guarantor for others that accepting power is the right thing to do. As such, the teacher is a midwife, assisting at a birth. The teacher is Annie Sullivan tapping the letters w-a-t-e-r into Helen's hand over and over and over again, convinced that she **has** the capacity and ability.[30] The teacher is the Apollinaire of Christopher Logue's poem, calling

"Come to the edge."
It's too high.

"Come to the edge."
We might fall.

COME TO THE EDGE.
And they came.
And she pushed them.
And they flew.[31]

And in a spirituality of teaching, the teacher is also a kind of priest, ordaining the learner into a world of responsibility. Dwelling in such a relation, women—and men and children too—can accept power and know the moment of ordination into it in response, feeling themselves close to Shange's Lady in Purple, who acknowledges "A layin' of hands: the holiness of myself released."[32] This is the grace of power which a spirituality of teaching leads to: recognizing the holiness and power of ourselves released and sent forth into the world.

RELEASE

Which brings us to the last pedagogical turn in the step of Revelation, release. This time, however, it is not the learner's release of power, but the teacher's release of the learner which is involved. In a careful examination of the act of teaching in *Religious Body*, Gabriel Moran makes the point, "at precisely the right moment, the teacher must let go."[33] Two elements are critical here: the need for a sense of timing and the act of letting go.

We have not spoken at all about those philosophies of education which say there is no need for a
teacher—philosophies which prefer terms like facili-
tator, guide, friend or coach—and look on teaching,
much as we saw with power—as a dirty word. For our
view is based on the conviction that Pedagogy continues to be a universal human concern, and teachers and
teaching are necessary for individuals and societies.
Still the paradox in the teacher's role is that it becomes
perfected—complete—when the teacher is no longer
needed, and when the phrase "Hands off" is the only
appropriate one. Having assisted people through embodiment toward revelation and the grace of power,
the teacher now moves aside in order to let that power
develop. An analogy with the artistic work of a sculptor molding clay can help.

When we form new life out of clay, and achieve a
completed vessel, a great temptation confronts us. We
find ourselves tempted to keep on working, to make
one more line, to add one more design, to deepen one
last hollow. When this happens, it is important to be
aware of the moment in the creative act of molding, as
in the spirituality of teaching, where a person must
say, "I can do no more," and where the only appropriate thing to do is let go. To do otherwise is to claim
time—a present and a future—which is not ours to
claim. For the other is on her or his own, and the
movement now demanded of the teacher is cessation
of movement, or rest, or emptiness.

I would argue for the spirituality of this moment
of release because of its echoes in the religious life of
the world. Release is close to **satori**, the absence of de-

sire and the fulfillment of desire at the same time. It is close to the Zen art of archery: in Zen the archer and arrow are one, here subject and subject have become one. It is also close to the *Hsing-Hsing Ming* of Zen, which says that when you try to be quiet by stopping activity, the quiet you achieve is in motion. It is akin to the full rest of sabbath, where the cessation of movement re-creates the world, and to **kenosis**, the full emptiness of Jesus of Nazareth in becoming accepting of death. It is the moment of simplicity—the complete simplicity of T.S. Eliot 'costing no less than everything.'

Still release, although the last moment in the work of Artistry, is not the ending or last step of pedagogy. For although it is a moment of rest, emptiness and stillness it is so that out of it a new step may come into being—the step toward which all teaching moves. This is the step where New Being comes into the world, New Life makes itself heard, and New Creation takes on its own identity. The teacher is still present, assisting and encouraging, but the main work now belongs to the other. This is the step of Birthing.

THEMES FOR A SPIRITUALITY
OF PEDAGOGY

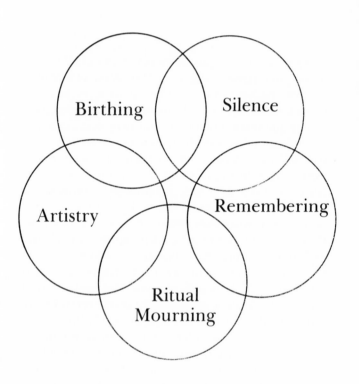

5:
BIRTHING

"Pregnant and birthing mothers are elemental forces, in the same sense that gravity, thunderstorms, earthquakes, and hurricanes are elemental forces. In order to understand the laws of their energy flow, you have to love and respect them for their magnificence at the same time that you study them with the accuracy of a true scientist." So writes Ina Gaskin, in *Spiritual Midwifery,*[1] introducing us to the last of our themes. For Birthing, used as a step in pedagogy, envisions a learner as an elemental force, bearing within the power to recreate everything: the self, the universe, God. It is not a power to be taken lightly, nor is it limited to women bearing children; it is a human power possessed by women and men and children as well as other animals. It is also a poetic and metaphorical power, which can be brought to bear on everything we touch. In this final section, we will study birthing in three ways. First, we will examine some of the meanings of birthing itself, and then we will look at birthing within pedagogy. Finally, we will suggest some of the broader relations between birthing and a spirituality of teaching, set in the world beyond pedagogy.

In 1923, economist Charlotte Perkins Gilman proposed two fundamentally different life orientations: one based on death, the other based on birth. She saw these orientations as the foundations of religion, writing,

> For the death-based religion, the main question is 'What is going to happen to me after I am dead?'—a posthumous egoism. To the birth-based religion, the main question is, 'What is to be done for the child who is born?' an immediate altruism. . . . The death-based religions have led to a limitless individualism, a demand for the eternal extension of personality. . . . The birth-based religion is necessarily and essentially altruistic, a forgetting of oneself for the good of the child, and tends to develop naturally into love and labor for the widening range of family, state and world.[2]

While I would take issue with Gilman in making such a sharp distinction, believing instead that the reality is birth *and* death (since all creation is born, grows, declines and dies) I do agree with her that we have not concentrated on the great power birth has to teach us about our worlds. Much education, especially, *has* been death-based, in the sense that competitiveness, narrowness of vision and refusal of admittance to the outsider has led to a limitless individualism and a demand for the eternal extension of personality. By failing to concentrate on the lives of women we have not developed naturally toward love and labor for the human family, the state and the world. We have kept ourselves not from the pain of death, but from the pain of birth. However, if we situate Birthing as a generative theme in pedagogy, we can learn new ways to explore the uncharted places of the geography of teaching, especially the directions toward which a spirituality of teaching leads.

Another woman who has examined the meanings of Birthing, as well as the accompanying experiences of nursing, aging and the wisdom of women's bodies, is Stephanie Demetrakopoulos. Her work is called *Listening to Our Bodies: The Rebirth of Feminine Wisdom,* and is an extensive consideration of birth using scientific, anthropological, metaphysical and religious sources as well as her own experience.[3] For example, she gives in detail an illuminating commentary on the work of Stanislav Grof, who names four stages of birth—oceanic unity with the mother, entrapment in the birth canal as labor begins, the actual birth, and the sense of a new kind of universal bliss after birth.[4] These stages are presented as analogues in later life for any extremely intense experience. But she also draws on her own reflective life. "When I look at my oldest daughter," she writes, "now twenty-five, I feel the oddest metaphysical start or shock to realize that this adult person is the same burrowing, suckling creature I nursed so many years ago."[5] But then she draws an implication which has pertinence to our pedagogical themes.

This gives me a special tenderness toward all adults, as I can psychically unpeel the layers of maturity and see the needy and vulnerable infant that all of the adult unfolding builds from and covers over. Perhaps women, through caring for infants and especially through the very concrete act of nursing, have a sense of the primordial seed in each person and of the mystery of human development which is often harder for men to come by.[6]

Undoubtedly women, even women who have not borne children, do have such a sense. Men might not have such knowing first hand. Still, especially if we would admit birthing as a universal theme, it would be a mistake to believe that men are incapable of sharing this sense with women, especially the many intuitive and non-patriarchal men who desire for themselves and all people the kind of teaching we have been describing. And perhaps the thing that will convert some other men, as Regina Coll notes, is a gradual realization of the processes they have not considered—such as Birthing—"the realization that their minds have not been fully developed because of the negative ideas we have about the body; that men do not know what they are capable of becoming because so-called feminine qualities are denigrated."[7] Perhaps if such qualities are developed, both men and women can then celebrate the following insight:

When a child is born, the entire Universe has to shift and make room. Another entity capable of free will, and therefore capable of becoming God, has been born. In that way, every child's birth is exactly like the birth of a world teacher. Every child born is a living Buddha.[8]

BIRTHING WITHIN PEDAGOGY

Although Birthing is a step in pedagogy which affects both teachers and learners, its major focus is toward the student—the person who is experiencing herself or himself as subject, as a receptor of the grace of power—coming to birth. And the first thing Birthing tells us about this moment is the wisdom of taking time, corroborating the insights of Release. (I am using the term Birthing in this chapter rather than 'Birth' to emphasize its processive, ongoing character.) Human birth takes nine months. It refuses to be hurried. And so for teachers and for students who want to know everything now, whether that now is the fourth grade or upon conferral of the Ph.D., this can be a liberating notion. Semesters and grades and courses can be understood as openings and beginnings where seeds are planted. But the moment of revelatory Birthing comes in its own time, in the healthy unhurriedness of the process.

Human Birthing also takes place in hiddenness. Even though our sophisticated technology gives us all kinds of clues about the future of the organism, the daily movement into Birthing occurs in darkness. All good pedagogy conveys this, and a teacher who can remind us of this is the wise and hard-working L.C. Moffat of Emlyn Williams' great play, *The Corn Is Green*. In the first part of the play, Moffat has been completely discouraged by her attempts to teach the children and young people of a small mining community in Wales. Her baggage is ready to be picked up, and she has assumed her efforts ended, stillborn. But as she is leaving, she notices a set of papers, crudely written by one group of boys. She stops, startled, at one of them, and we listen as she reads the young miner Morgan Evans' first attempt at writing:

> The mine is dark . . . if a light come in the mine . . . the rivers in the mine will run fast with the voice of many women; the walls will fall in and it will be the end of the world. So the mine is dark. . . . But when I walk through the Tan shaft in the dark, I can touch with my hands the trees, and underneath where the corn is green. . . . [9]

Moffat then works with Evans in a metaphoric, comparative process, trying to discover where her own teaching might continue to assist birth in this slowly greening human being. Still it must be noted that it was the learner, the young Morgan Evans, who had the initial intuition concerning Birthing. He too was wise, wise enough to realize that somewhere birth was happening; somewhere the corn was green. And we, learners and teachers everywhere, can imitate them whenever we take Birthing seriously as a major step in pedagogy, learning to value its hiddenness.

The literature of teaching is once again incorporating such insights so that they provide counsel for pedagogy as it moves from Artistry to Birthing. One such insight (reappropriated from Socrates) is that as students come more and more into the possession of themselves, and the teacher moves more to the side, the pedagogical role shifts toward Midwifery. But what needs to be stressed at this point is that the role of Midwife is the community's, even more than it is that of the individual teacher. The teacher has assisted the learner in coming to this point. But when Birthing is happening, the circumstances in the environment and the wider community—be it in an institution such as school, church or family, or a broader setting such as city, state or nation—ought to alert everyone to the role of Midwife-Teacher. And this broader commitment—to which we will return—is particularly critical for empowering women who have only recently moved through Silence, Remembering, Mourning and Artistry. In *Women's Ways of Knowing,* we are given several characteristics of this role:

> *Item:* Midwife-teachers assist others in giving birth to their own ideas, in drawing them out, in making the others' own tacit knowledge explicit and elaborating it.

> *Item:* Midwife-teachers do not administer anesthesia. They support the persons' think-

ing but they do not do the thinking for them
or expect the persons to think as they do.

Item: Midwife-teachers' first concern is to
preserve the others' fragile newborn
thoughts, to see that they are born with their
truth intact, that they do not turn into ac-
ceptable lies.

Item: Midwife-teachers focus not on their
own knowledge but on the others' knowledge. To them, the baby is not theirs, but the
other persons'.[10]

To expect such commitment to Birthing on the
part of the wider community may be naive, but it is not
impossible. And no reason exists why it cannot be suggested and celebrated as a social ideal. One way to do
this lies in considering models who have demonstrated a knowledge of exactly what is involved. From
all accounts that we have of her, one of the great Midwife Teachers in religious education of this century
was Nelle Morton, who died in July of 1987 and who
embodied in her teaching all of the themes in this
book. In a reminiscence which talked about birth, and
in what is yet another reflection on speech, hearing
and voice, she spoke for both teachers and learners at
the step of Birthing; she also spoke for the broader
society:

Once we took the painful journey to the core
of our lives, we found that we were sustained.

In the awful loneliness, we were not alone. Something shaped our cry—brought forth our speech, fragmentary as it was. We had been told all our lives that the word created, that the word came first—even in the beginning, before the beginning. Now we know a priority to the word—a hearing that brought forth the word. We literally heard one another down to a word that was **our** word, and that word was ourselves.

Hearing, as we have come to experience it, proceeds not from a collective ear that would suggest an aggregate, but from a great ear at the heart of the universe hearing persons to humanness. And the humanness is marked by wholeness (the whole word, and not just the masculine word). In the morphology—down, then up from down under—we have experienced *birth,* not rebirth, not new birth, or rite of passage or entry, but *birth* of ourselves for the first time. We have experienced creation, not re-creation, or new creation, but a primordial creation of ourselves. In the new shape of our experience, we have confronted death, but not death of the self, or death to self. We have experienced the death of the stereotyped images, the breaking of them from within so that self can be affirmed and potentialized.[11]

Still, with all this testimony, it needs to be said that some birth is stillborn, that other births are aborted and not allowed to occur—for whatever reason—and that birth always entails pain. Writing of Women's Studies in Argentina, for example, Gloria Bonder notes that in their learning women went through three phases: an encyclopedic phase which begins in a celebration of scientific knowledge and ends in disillusion with it; a transitional phase of awakening to the reality of women's subordination within all knowledge, with the need to create a new model; and a third phase, which rather than being called birthing is better named "dilemmatic"—where there are bitter feelings of defeat in the face of established knowledge set vis-à-vis the conviction that women's subjectivity is expressed in another kind of symbol.[12] And the new models are not created yet; the birthing has not yet happened, and we cannot be sure it will. We can only hope and work in that direction.

BIRTHING BEYOND PEDAGOGY

Such a set of realities poses demanding questions to both learners and teachers completing this last step. What are we bearing? What are we baring or revealing? Birthing tells us that we bear bodiliness, enfleshment, new life, passion, emotion, feeling, blood, water, and pain. Birthing tells us of our human radiance, and sees people of all ages clad in splendor, even if, as Thomas Merton wrote, "There is no way of telling people that they are all walking around shining like the sun."[13] Birthing tells us that we also bear responsibility: **for** ourselves, **to** other selves, and **for** the young, the animals and the earth who may need our voices and our listening. Birthing tells us that we bear responsibility for the systems and structures and institutions that make life possible for the world and its inhabitants. And so it impels us into other arenas. It forces us to listen to the question, "What is our Birthing toward?"

We have already begun to suggest directions this answer might take in proposing that the real Midwife-Teacher in Birthing is the community. The point to be made here is that all of the steps we have proposed in a spirituality of teaching are set in a wider context. To assume the work is only interpersonal, between a teacher and a student, is to make a fundamental mistake. For all the persons involved in the activities we have named work in environments which either enhance and encourage or impede and frustrate. Thus, one of the very first Birthings beyond Pedagogy is of places, settings, and situations where the issues and processes of women and pedagogy are taken seriously. This demands the involvement of administrators, financial officers, legislators and other leaders. It demands the awareness of a spirituality of teaching based on the premise that all institutions teach by the kind of places they *are*. It also demands a recognition of just how fundamental the desired changes will be.

A related Birthing here is the acknowledgement and attentiveness to places other than schools where teaching goes on. Obviously, the major analogue for teaching I have used in this essay is the schoolteacher, and the major setting to which I have drawn attention is the school. But if the process of pedagogy described here is valid, if it is **right**, then this process ought to be encouraged wherever teaching goes on. That means it needs to be extended and encouraged and birthed in families, at the work place, and, notably, in churches, synagogues, temples and religiously-affiliated settings such as retreat centers, houses of prayer, revivals and missions.

Such a set of steps needs to be encouraged in the wider society too, calling that society to the continuing work of justice. For if a pedagogy which takes women students seriously is to have a chance, and if such a pedagogy is also appropriate for all people, then the conditions which enable justice to occur must be created and enabled in the broader social, political, and economic contexts where teaching happens. And although the first birth **is** of the person,[14] any pedagogy which stops at the Birthing of oneself is simply too narrow for our time. Birthing must spill over to the Birthing of just environments in society itself, for Birth and Breakthrough, as Meister Eckhart taught, are "resurrections into justice."[15]

The conditions which enable justice to occur have not changed since Isaiah, although the need for their Birthing may have grown more urgent. They are still elements in the fast described by the prophet:

Is not this the sort of fast that pleases me
—it is the Lord Yahweh who speaks—

to break unjust fetters and undo the thongs of
    the yoke,
to let the oppressed go free
and break every yoke,
to share your bread with the hungry
and shelter the homeless poor,
to clothe the one you see to be naked
and not turn from your own kin?
Then will your light shine like the dawn
and your wound be quickly healed over.
Your integrity will go before you
and the glory of Yahweh behind you.
Cry, and Yahweh will answer;
call, and Yahweh will say, "I am here."

(Is 58:6–9)

Yet, although the conditions for justice have not
changed, the quality and sound of the voice of Yahweh has. For throughout the world, as the hungry, the
homeless poor, the naked and the oppressed continue
to be disproportionately women and girls, the female
face of the divine and the female sound of her voice
has begun to resonate. The image of God calling for
justice is the girlchild as well as the boychild, the
mother as well as the father, the Christa as well as the
Christ. And in her call and her cry we come to one last
Birthing—the Birthing of a divinity who is Mother as
well as Father, Goddess as well as God, Sister as well
as Brother, Child as well as Parent, Earth as well as
Heaven. An Unnameable One beyond all images in
the end, yes, but One who contains within the Divine
Self all the wisdom, all the wholeness, all the compas-

sion, all the justice we seek. One who reminds us, as Meister Eckhart also taught, that "We are all meant to be mothers of God. For God is always needing to be born."[16]

In that last remembering, we are brought full circle to the beginning of the dance. For Birthing, although the last step, is not the culminating moment in pedagogy or in a spirituality of teaching. There is no last moment. Instead, there is a continuing dance and a continuing rhythm, where artistry blends into remembering as well as into birthing, where mourning appears in the midst of silence as well as after remembering, and where silence itself belongs in all the other themes. And the reason the rhythm must continue, quite simply, is due to the demands of the present. Due to the situation. The rhythm of pedagogy must continue because none of us can be free until all are free. Because there is no justice for one of us unless there is justice for all of us. And so a spirituality of teaching pauses here, although it does not cease. It pauses because it must take time for quiet, peace and reconciliation in order to become aware of disquiet, the absence of peace, and the disharmony in our midst. And in the pause, a blessing is heard, spoken by the millions of voices who have unlearned their not-speaking; a blessing which can serve as our accompanying music as we find ourselves once more at the beginning step of silence; a blessing upon our work as teachers. The blessing is, as blessing, both our vespers and our matins, our evening and our daybreak:

May your heart's disquiet never vanish;
May you never be at peace;
May you never be reconciled to life,
    nor to death either;
May your steps be unending. . . . [17]

Introduction: Impulses

1. Sister M. Madeleva Wolff. *My First Seventy Years* (New York: Macmillan, 1959), pp. 5–6.
2. See Anne Wilson Schaef, *Women's Reality,* for a discussion of the differences between forms natural and unnatural to women (Minneapolis: Winston, 1981).
3. Madeleva, *op. cit.,* p. 6. The notion of forms as "foreign" or unnatural is not, of course, limited to the experience of women. Mexican-American Virgil Elizondo, for example, speaks of the foreignness of much of his early education as one where the forms were not his own.
4. For a celebration of untapped forms of knowing, see Jerome Bruner, *On Knowing. Essays for the Left Hand* (Cambridge: Harvard University Press, 1962).
5. Bill Maroon, in an unpublished paper.
6. Chicago: Follett Publishing Co., 1980.
7. Malcolm Knowles. *The Adult Learner: A Neglected Species* (Houston: Gulf Publishing Co., 1973).
8. Knowles, *Modern Practice . . . ,* pp. 43–44.
9. New York: Herder and Herder, 1970.
10. *Ibid.,* p. 33.
11. *Ibid.*
12. *Ibid.*
13. See Jean Baker Miller, *Toward a New Psychology of Women,* 2nd ed. (Boston: Beacon, 1986); Carol Gilligan, *In a Different Voice* (Cambridge: Harvard University

Press, 1982); Nancy Chodorow, *The Reproduction of Mothering* (Berkeley: University of California Press, 1978).

14. New Haven: Yale University Press, 1985.
15. New York: Basic Books, 1986.
16. New York: Harcourt Brace Jovanovich, 1957 (1929).
17. New York: Harcourt Brace Jovanovich, 1966 (1938).
18. In *On Lies, Secrets and Silence* (New York: W.W. Norton and Co., 1979), pp. 231–236, 237–246.
19. Gerda Lerner. *The Majority Finds Its Past* (New York: Oxford University Press, 1979).
20. *Op. cit.*, pp. 240–241.
21. *Ibid.*, p. 242.
22. *Ibid.*, pp. 243–244.
23. University of Chicago Press, 5801 Ellis Avenue, Chicago, Ill. 60637.
24. Women's Studies Program, University of Maryland, College Park, Md. 20742.
25. Pergamon Press, Fairview Park, Elmsford, N.Y. 10523.
26. In "Spiritual Quest and Women's Experience," in *Womanspirit Rising*, edited by Carol P. Christ and Judith Plaskow (New York: Harper and Row, 1979), p. 230.
27. In *Women and Spirituality* (Totowa, New Jersey: Rowman and Allenheld, 1983).
28. Rosemary Ruether, "Feminist Theology and Spirituality," in Judith Weidman (ed.), *Christian Feminism* (San Francisco: Harper and Row, 1984), p. 14.
29. See Matthew Fox, *Original Blessing* (Santa Fe: Bear and Co., 1983).
30. See *Western Spirituality: Historical Roots, Ecumenical Routes*, edited by Matthew Fox (Santa Fe: Bear and Co., 1981), p. 2.
31. In *The Awful Rowing Towards God* (Boston: Houghton Mifflin, 1975), p. 83.

32. See *To Know as We Are Known. A Spirituality of Education* (San Francisco: Harper and Row, 1983), p. 68.

33. *Ibid.,* p. 65.

34. *Op. cit.,* p. 18.

35. See Suzanne Langer, *Mind: An Essay on Human Feeling* (Baltimore: The Johns Hopkins Press, 1967).

36. John Dewey, *Art as Experience* (New York: Capricorn Books, 1958 [1934]). See pp. 147ff.

37. Alfred North Whitehead, *The Aims of Education* (New York: Macmillan, 1929), pp. 15–28.

38. *Op. cit.,* pp. 79–118.

39. See James Fowler. *Stages of Faith* (San Francisco: Harper and Row, 1981).

40. See Gabriel Moran. *No Ladder to the Sky* (San Francisco: Harper and Row, 1987).

41. I am indebted to Judith Dorney for this metaphor and the accompanying insights.

1: Silence

1. New York: Delacorte Press, 1978.

2. *Op. cit.*

3. Nancy A. Falk and Rita M. Gross (eds.), *Unspoken Worlds: Women's Religious Lives in Non-Western Cultures* (San Francisco: Harper and Row, 1980).

4. *Op. cit.*

5. *Op. cit.*

6. Boston: Beacon, 1987.

7. Boston: Beacon, 1987.

8. *Op. cit.*

9. *Ibid.,* p. 18.

10. *Ibid.*

11. New York: Macmillan, 1985 (1979), 2nd ed., pp. 87–108. The null curriculum corresponds to what some educators refer to as "excluded knowledge."

12. Gloria Steinem, "The Politics of Talking in Groups," in *Ms.* 9 (May 1981), pp. 43, 45, 84, 86–89.
13. *Op. cit.*
14. Jean-Jacques Rousseau, *Emile*, trans. Allan Bloom (New York: Basic Books, 1979).
15. Martin, *op. cit.*
16. See Phyllis Trible's study of Hagar in *Texts of Terror* (Philadelphia: Fortress, 1984).
17. The question is Kathryn Allen Rabuzzi's. See her *The Sacred and the Feminine: Toward a Theology of Housework* (New York: Seabury, 1982), p. 155.
18. *Op. cit.*, pp. 29–39.
19. In Christ and Plaskow, *op. cit.*, pp. 25–42.
20. *Ibid.*, p. 37.
21. For syllabi and courses which meet this loss, see Gloria T. Hull, Patricia Bell Scott and Barbara Smith, *All the Women Are White, All the Blacks Are Men, But Some of Us Are Brave* (Old Westbury, N.Y.: The Feminist Press, 1982).
22. In an unpublished manuscript entitled, "Lost, Hidden or Broken Images."
23. In "Spiritual Quest . . ." *op. cit.*, p. 230.
24. See n. 32, above.
25. New York: Simon and Schuster, 1972, pp. 222–223.
26. In "Taking Women Students Seriously," *op. cit.*, p. 244.
27. *Ibid.*
28. In *for colored girls who have considered suicide/when the rainbow is enuf* (New York: Macmillan, 1976), p. 66.
29. *Op. cit.*; see especially p. 182.

2: Remembering

1. Catherine Keller, *From a Broken Web. Separation, Sexism and Self* (Boston: Beacon, 1986), p. 67. I am indebted to Keller for much in this section.

2. *Ibid.*

3. *Ibid.*

4. "While love is unfashionable," in *Revolutionary Petunias and Other Poems* (New York: Harcourt Brace Jovanovich, 1973), p. 68.

5. In *Pure Lust* (Boston: Beacon, 1984), p. 175.

6. New York: The Seabury Press, 1980, pp. 109–110.

7. Mary Daly, *Gyn/Ecology: The Metaethics of Radical Feminism* (Boston: Beacon, 1978).

8. Andrea Dworkin, *Woman Hating: A Radical Look at Sexuality* (New York: E.P. Dutton, 1976).

9. *Ibid.*, p. 95.

10. See Carolyn Osiek, *Beyond Anger* (New York: Paulist Press, 1986), pp. 71–72.

11. Dorothee Soelle, *Suffering* (Philadelphia: Fortress, 1975), pp. 70–73.

12. Madeleva, *op. cit.*, pp. 110–113.

13. See, for example, Mary Perkins Ryan, *Speaking of How to Pray* (New York: Sheed and Ward, 1948); Mary Perkins Ryan, editor and translator of Jean Daniélou, *The Bible and the Liturgy* (Notre Dame: University of Notre Dame, 1956) and of Louis Bouyer *The Meaning of Sacred Scripture* (Notre Dame: University of Notre Dame, 1958); as well as her *Are Parochial Schools the Answer?* (Boston: St. Paul Editions, 1964) and *We're All in This Together* (New York: Holt, Rinehart and Winston, 1972).

14. See Nathan Jones, *Sharing the Old, Old Story. Educational Ministry in the Black Community* (Winona: St. Mary's Press, 1982), pp. 62–63.

15. See Molly Rush, "Living, Mothering, Resisting," in *Christianity and Crisis* (December 8, 1980), pp. 348; and Liane Ellison Norman, "Living Up to Molly," *ibid.*, pp. 341–344.

16. See John Simpson and Jana Bennett, *The Disappeared and the Mothers of the Plaza: The Story of the 11,000 Argentinians Who Vanished* (New York: St. Martin's Press, 1985).

17. In Guy Brett, *Through Our Own Eyes. Popular Art and Modern History* (Philadelphia: New Society Publishers, 1987), 149.

18. See Maria Harris, "Isms and Religious Education," in *Emerging Issues in Religious Education,* Gloria Durka and Joanmarie Smith (eds.) (New York: Paulist, 1976), pp. 40–57, for a development of the communal nature of remembering.

19. See Margot Strom and William Parsons, *Facing History and Ourselves. Holocaust and Human Behavior* for a curriculum which does face this issue (Watertown, Mass.: Intentional Publications, 1982).

20. In *Pintig. Lifepulse in Cold Steel. Poems and Letters from Philippine Prison* (Kowloon, Hong Kong: Resource Center for Philippine Concerns, 1979), p. 118.

21. See Maria Harris, *Teaching and Religious Imagination* (San Francisco: Harper and Row, 1987), pp. 50–54.

22. Maria Harris, "Fantasy: Entrance into Inwardness," in *British Journal of Religious Education,* 10, 1 (Autumn 1987), p. 10.

23. Rom 8:19–23.

24. Karl Rahner and Herbert Vorgrimler, "Anamnesis," in *Theological Dictionary* (New York: Herder and Herder, 1965), pp. 19–20.

25. New York: The Pilgrim Press, 1981.

26. Janet Kalven and Mary I. Buckley (eds.), *Women's Spirit Bonding* (New York: The Pilgrim Press, 1984).

27. Rosemary Radford Ruether. *WomanGuides: Readings Toward a Feminist Theology* (Boston: Beacon Press, 1985).

28. Trumansburg, N.Y.: The Crossing Press, 1981.

29. 8035 13th Street, Silver Spring, Md. 20910.

30. Judy Chicago, *The Dinner Party* (New York: Doubleday, 1979).

3: Ritual Mourning

1. Judy Collins, "Bread and Roses," on *The First Fifteen Years* (Los Angeles: Elektra/Asylum Records, 1975).

2. John Keats, "Hyperion," in Book III of *The Complete Works of Keats* (Boston: Houghton Mifflin, Cambridge Edition, 1899), 8th printing, 211–212.

3. Erich Lindemann, "Symptomatology and Management of Acute Grief," in Robert Fulton, ed., *Death and Identity* (New York: John Wiley and Sons, Inc. 1965), 186–201. Reprinted from *American Journal of Psychiatry* 101 (1944), 141–148. See also Geoffrey Gorer, *Death, Grief and Mourning* (London: The Cresset Press, 1965).

4. See Elisabeth Kübler-Ross, *On Death and Dying* (New York: Macmillan, 1969).

5. "The Power of Anger in the Work of Love: Christian Ethics for Women and Other Strangers," in *Union Theological Seminary Review* (Supplementary, 1981), p. 49.

6. *Ibid.*

7. Jean Shinoda Bolen, *Goddesses in Everywoman* (San Francisco: Harper and Row, 1984), pp. 288–289.

8. Osiek, *op. cit.*, pp. 16ff, 24.

9. Edwina Hunter, "Reflections on the Christa from a Christian Theologian," in *Journal of Women and Religion*, 4, 2 (Winter 1985), p. 31.

10. See Buckley and Kalven, *op. cit.*

11. *Ibid.*, pp. 65–66.

12. Katie Cannon, *et al.* (The Mudflower Collective), *God's Fierce Whimsy. Christian Feminism and Theological Education* (New York: The Pilgrim Press, 1985).

13. Albert Camus, *The Rebel* (New York: Knopf, 1967), p. 28. First published 1956.
14. See Abraham Heschel, *The Prophets* (New York: Harper and Row, 1962), Vol. 2, pp. 1–58.
15. See Matthew Fox, *Compassion* (Minneapolis: Winston Press, 1979), pp. 10–14.
16. See Walter Brueggemann, in "Voices of the Night—Against Justice," pp. 5–28, in Walter Brueggemann, Sharon Parks and Thomas H. Groome, *To Act Justly, Love Tenderly, Walk Humbly* (New York: Paulist Press, 1986).
17. Harrison, *op. cit.*, p. 50.
18. Belenky *et al.*, *op. cit.* p. 130.
19. Marge Piercy, "Unlearning to Not Speak," in *To Be of Use* (New York: Doubleday, 1973), p. 38.
20. In "Women's Rites," in *Vogue*, 170, 9 (September 1980), p. 514.
21. Letty Cottin Pogrebin, "Going Public as a Jew," in *Ms.* (July-August 1987), p. 195.
22. In 1987, drawing on a letter from their founder, Mother Catherine McAuley, who spoke of the passage through life as a dance called the "Grand Right and Left," the U.S. Mercy Sisters designed a "dance" where all the communities throughout the country gave and received artistic creations from one another, in a kind of ongoing, corporate dance.
23. In a personal communication.
24. "Sister," recorded by Cris Williamson on *The Changer and the Changed* (Oakland: Olivia Records, 1975).
25. "Singing for Our Lives," recorded by Holly Near and Ronnie Gilbert on *Lifeline* (Oakland: Redwood Records, 1983).

1. *Op. cit.*, p. 18.
2. Evelyn Keller and C.R. Grontkowski, "The Mind's Eye," cited in Belenky *et al.*, *op. cit.*
3. See my *Teaching and Religious Imagination, op. cit.*, especially chapters 1 and 9.
4. See Susanne Langer, *Problems of Art* (New York: Charles Scribner's Sons, 1957), p. 80.
5. In "Immanence: Uniting the Spiritual and Political," in Kalven and Buckley, *op. cit.*, p. 317.
6. These themes are developed at length as the major elements in a framework for teaching in my *Teaching and Religious Imagination.*
7. "Women and Theological Education: Changes in the Past Decade and New Questions," in *WTC Newsletter*, 5, 3 (September 1987), p. 1.
8. *Ibid.*, p. 2.
9. *Ibid.*, pp. 2, 4.
10. Margo Culley and Catherine Portuges (eds.), *Gendered Subjects. The Dynamics of Feminist Teaching* (Boston: Routledge and Kegan Paul, 1985).
11. Diedrick Snoek, "A Male Feminist in a Women's College Classroom," in Culley and Portuges, *op. cit.*, p. 138.
12. Michele Russell, "Black-eyed blues Connections: Teaching Black Women," in Culley and Portuges, *op. cit.*, pp. 155–168.
13. Barbara Gates, Susan Klaw and Adria Steinberg, *Changing Learning, Changing Lives: A High School Women's Studies Curriculum from the Group School* (Old Westbury, N.Y.: The Feminist Press, 1979).
14. Judith A. Dorney, "Religious Education and the Development of Young Women," in Fern M. Giltner (ed.),

Women's Issues in Religious Education (Birmingham: Religious Education Press, 1985), pp. 41–65.

15. Regina Coll, "Education for Peace: A Feminist Issue," in Giltner, *op. cit.*, p. 75.

16. In Charlotte Bunch and Sandra Pollack (eds.), *Learning Our Way. Essays in Feminist Education* (Trumansburg, N.Y.: The Crossing Press, 1983), pp. 261–271.

17. Washington: American Historical Association, 1981, pp. 15–21: 400 A Street S.E., Washington D.C. 20003.

18. See Gabriel Moran, *Theology of Revelation* (New York: Herder and Herder, 1966); *Catechesis of Revelation* (New York: Herder and Herder 1966); *The Present Revelation* (New York: Herder and Herder, 1972).

19. William Walsh, *The Use of Imagination.* (New York: Barnes and Noble, 1960), pp. 55–56.

20. See *Pedagogy of the Oppressed*, pp. 12–13, 20ff.

21. *Ibid.*

22. The phrase "indirect communication" is best known for its use by Soren Kierkegaard. See my *Teaching and Religious Imagination*, especially chapter 4 for application of the theme to teaching.

23. The distinction between expressive language and steno-language is Philip Wheelwright's. See his *The Burning Fountain* (Gloucester: Peter Smith, 1982), ch. 2. First published 1968.

24. Alice Walker, *The Color Purple* (New York: Washington Square Press, 1982), p. 247.

25. The distinction is Brian Wren's. See his *Education for Justice* (Maryknoll: Orbis, 1977). See also Paulo Freire, *Education for Critical Consciousness* (New York: Seabury, 1973).

26. Belenky et al., *op. cit.*, pp. 188–189.

27. *Ibid.*, p. 189.

28. See Rainer Maria Rilke, *Letters to a Young Poet* (New York: W.W. Norton, 1934), p. 33.

29. For development of the theme of responsibility and its relation to listening and speech, see Gabriel Moran, *No Ladder to the Sky,* especially pp. 66–83.

30. See Helen Keller, *The Story of My Life* (Garden City: Doubleday, 1936), pp. 23–24.

31. Adapted from *Ode to the Dodo. Poems from 1953 to 1978.* London: Cape, 1981, p. 96.

32. *Op. cit.,* p. 66.

33. New York; Seabury, 1974, p. 163.

5: *Birthing*

1. Summertown, Tenn.: The Book Publishing Co., 1977, pp. 282–283.

2. Quoted in Rosemary Radford Ruether, *Sexism and God Talk* (Boston: Beacon Press, 1983), p. 236.

3. Boston: Beacon Press, 1983.

4. *Ibid.,* pp. 20–29.

5. *Ibid.,* p. 34.

6. *Ibid.,* pp. 34–35.

7. *Op. cit.,* p. 72.

8. Ina Gaskin, *op. cit.*

9. *The Corn Is Green* in Emlyn Williams, *The Collected Plays,* Vol. 1 (New York: Random House, 1961), p. 263 (1938). I thank Catherine Chiffelle, with whom I team-taught several years, for alerting me to these meanings of teaching.

10. *Op. cit.,* pp. 217–219.

11. Nelle Morton, "The Dilemma of Celebration," in Christ and Plaskow, *op. cit.,* pp. 164–165.

12. Gloria Bonder, "The Educational Process of Women's Studies in Argentina: Reflections on Theory and Technique," in Culley and Portuges, *op. cit.,* pp. 70–77.

13. Quoted in Michael Mott, *The Seven Mountains of Thomas Merton* (Boston: Houghton Mifflin, 1984), p. 312.

14. *Breakthrough. Meister Eckhart's Creation Spirituality in New Translation.* Introduction and Commentaries by Matthew Fox (Garden City: Doubleday, 1980), p. 292.

15. *Ibid.*, p. 467.

16. Matthew Fox, *Original Blessing, op. cit.*, p. 222.

17. Adapted from Par Lagerkvist, *Evening Land/Aftonland*, translated by W.H. Auden and Leif Sjoberg (London: Souvenir Press, 1977), p. 141 (1953).

INDEX

Abraham   21
Aims of Education, The   94
alienation   26
anamnesis   42, 43
andragogy   5
anger   8, 44, 46, 49, 50, 51, 55, 56
Antigone   57
art of teaching   4, 6, 34, 60–75
artistry   16, 60–75, 90
Athena   34
Atwood, Margaret   28
Auschwitz   55
Awful Rowing Toward God, The   93, n31

Beecher, Catherine   7
Belenky, Mary   7, 70, 84
Bergen-Belsen   55
birth, and teaching   6, 15, 16, 72, 77–91
birthing   16, 77–91
body   11, 32, 34, 48, 62, 63, 79, 80, 86
Bolen, Jean Shinoda   98, n7
Bonder, Gloria   86
Boyd, Arthur   37
brokenness   11, 55
Brueggemann, Walter   99, n16

Bruner, Jerome   92, n4
Buckley, Mary   44
Bunch, Charlotte   101, n16

Camus, Albert   99, n13
Cannon, Katie   98, n12
Chicago, Judy   44
Chiffelle, Catherine   102, n9
children,   39
Chodorow, Nancy   7
Christ, Carol   10, 26, 27
Christa, the   37, 51, 52, 89
Cingari, Rosemary   25–26
Clark, Linda   44
Clinchy, Blythe   7, 70, 84
Cocoanut Grove Nightclub 48
Coll, Regina   58, 65–66, 80
Collins, Judy   47
Color Purple, The   69–70
community   39–42, 50, 51–53, 57, 66, 69, 83–84
context of teaching   7–8
Corn Is Green, The   82
Creation Spirituality   11
Culley, Margo   63–64
curriculum   7, 19, 62–67; explicit curriculum   19; implicit curriculum   19–20; null curriculum   19–21, 25

Daly, Mary   33, 35–36
dance steps   14–15, 45, 90–91

death   47, 51, 78, 79
Demetrakopoulos,
   Stephanie   79–80
desaparacidos   39
Dewey, John   13
Dinner Party, The   44, 55
Dorney, Judith   65, 94, n41
du Plessix Gray, Francine   57
Durka, Gloria   97 n18
Dworkin, Andrea   35–36

earth   41, 42
Eckhart, Meister   88, 90
*Educational Imagination,
   The*   19
Eisner, Elliot   19
Elizondo, Virgil   92n3
embodiment   62–67
Emile   21
environment for learning   5,
   15, 24–25, 83, 87, 88
Erikson, Erik   14

Falk, Nancy   17
feeling   55, 63
Feminist Studies   9, 93n24
Fowler, James   14
Fox, Matthew   93 n29, 99n15
Freire, Paulo 6, 15, 68–69, 101
   n20, n21

Gaskin, Ina   77, 81, 102 n8
Gates, Barbara   100 n13
Gendered Subjects   63–65
generative themes   15, 79
Gertrude   21
Gilbert, Ronnie   58
Gilligan, Carol   7, 17

Gilman, Charlotte Perkins   7,
   78
God's Fierce Whimsy   53
Goldberger, Nancy   7, 70, 84
Greenham Common   39
Grof, Stanislav   79
Gross, Rita   17

Hagar   21, 95 n16
Hamer, Fannie Lou   38
Harris, Maria   97 n18, n21,
   n22
Harrison, Beverly   49, 50, 56
healing   29–30, 34, 39, 57
hearing   84–85
Heschel, Abraham   54
Hildegard of Bingen   11
Holocaust   40–41
Hull, Gloria   95 n21
Hunter, Edwina   51–52

imagery   25, 37, 39, 43, 48,
   60, 89
In a Different Voice   17
indirect communication   69

Jackson, Jesse   72
Judeo-Christian tradition   24
Julian of Norwich   11
justice   38, 54–55, 88–90

Kalven, Janet   44
Keats, John   47
Keller, Catherine   32
Keller, Evelyn   60
Keller, Helen   72
Kierkegaard, Soren   101, n22

Klaw, Susan   100, n13
Knowles, Malcolm   5–6
Kohlberg, Lawrence   14
Kübler-Ross, Elisabeth   48–49
Kwok, Pui Lan   62

Lagerkvist, Par   103, n17
Langer, Susanne   61
Leonard   21
Lerner, Gerda   7, 66–67
Lindemann, Erich   48
listening   13, 29–30, 60, 72, 87
Logue, Christopher   72
loss, 25, 44, 48, 49, 50, 57

Mariechild, Diane   44
Maroon, Bill   92, n5
Martin, Jane Roland,   7, 17, 21
Martin, Theodora Penny   7
McAuley, Catherine   99, n22
Mead, Margaret   22
Mechtilde of Magdeburg   11
Medusa   33–34
memories of freedom   35
memories of suffering   35, 36
Merton, Thomas   86
Metz, John Baptist   35
midwifery   72, 77, 83–84
Miller, Jean Baker   7
Miriam   21, 26
Moran, Gabriel   73, 94, n40, 101, n18, 101–102, n29
Morton, Nelle   84–85
Moses   21, 26
mourning   16, 44–45, 46–59, 90

Mudflower Collective   98, n12
mythic remembering   32–34

naming   55
Near, Holly   58
Niebuhr, Reinhold   22
Nygren, Anders   22

Ochs, Carol   10, 15
Olsen, Tillie   17
original blessing   11
Osiek, Carolyn   51
Ostriker, Alicia Suskin   17

Palmer, Parker   13
Passover,   57
pedagogy   4–6, 15, 74, 86–91
   redesigning pedagogy   2, 47–48
Pedagogy of the Oppressed   6
Perseus   34
Pestalozzi, Johann   7, 21
Piaget, Jean   14
Piercy, Marge   56
Plaskow, Judith   93, n26
Plato   7
Plaza de Mayo   39
Pogrebin, Letty Cottin   57
Pollack, Sandra   101, n16
Portuges, Catherine   63
Poseidon   33
power   27–28, 29, 34, 71–73, 81
pride   22

questioning   69–70

Rabuzzi, Kathryn Allen   95, n17

Rahner, Karl   69
rebellion   53
receptivity   29, 62, 71–73, 81
Reclaiming a Conversation   7, 17
release   62, 73–75, 81
remembering   16, 31–45, 90; communal remembering 39–42; dangerous remembering 34–39; liturgical remembering 42–45; mythic remembering 32–34
responding   13, 72, 73
revelation   62, 67–70
rhythm   13–16, 90–91
Rich, Adrienne   7–9, 17, 28
Rilke, Rainer Maria   101, n28
ritual   44, 56–59
Ronan, Marian   44
Room of One's Own, A   7
Rousseau, Jean-Jacques   7, 21
Ruether, Rosemary   11, 13, 14, 44
Rush, Molly   38–39
Russell, Michelle   64–65
Ryan, Mary Perkins   38

sabbath   75
Saiving, Valerie   22–23
Sandys, Edwina   37
Sarah   21
Schaef, Anne Wilson   92, n2
Schniedewind, Nancy   66
Scott, Patricia Bell   95, n21
Sexton, Anne   12
Shange, Ntozake   29, 73
Shekinah   29
Signs   9, 93, n23

silence   8, 10, 16, 17–30, 75, 90
   contemplative silence   29–30
Smith, Barbara   95, n21
Smith, Joanmarie   97, n18
Snoek, Diedrick   100, n11
Soelle, Dorothee   37
sorrow   25, 44
speech   20, 56, 84
spirituality   10–13, spirituality of teaching   11, 12, 15, 30, 49, 54, 56, 61, 70, 73, 74, 75, 77, 87, 90
Starhawk, 62
Steinberg, Adria   100, n13
subject ontological vocation 68–69
subject matter   67–68
subjects, human   68
Sullivan, Annie   72

Tarule, Jill   7, 70, 84
teaching as religious   9–10, 43
Texts of Terror   95, n16
Three Guineas   7, 21–22

U.S. Sisters of Mercy   58

victim   28, 34
voice   8, 17, 18, 19, 31, 55, 57, 60, 84, 87, 89, 90

Walker, Alice   33
Walker, Eleanor   44
Walsh, William   101, n19
W.A.T.E.R.   44, 98, n29

Weidman, Judith   93, n28
Weng, Li-li   20
Wheelwright, Philip   101, n23
Whitehead, Alfred North   14
Williams, Emlyn   82
Williamson, Cris   58
Wolff, Madeleva (Eva)   1, 2, 38
Wollstonecraft, Mary   7
woman's seder   57
women of color   24, 38, 52–53, 64–65

women as students 6–10, 21–22
women's studies   9, 63–64, 65, 66, 67
Women's Studies International Forum   9, 93, n25
Women's Theological Center   62–63
Women's Ways of Knowing   7, 17–19, 60, 70, 83–84
Woolf, Virginia   7, 21–22, 30
Wren, Brian   101, n25